INNER HEALING FOR HOLES IN THE SOUL

Dr. Betty Mitchell

authorHOUSE®

AuthorHouse™
1663 Liberty Drive
Bloomington, IN 47403
www.authorhouse.com
Phone: 1-800-839-8640

First published by AuthorHouse 6/1/2010

ISBN: 978-1-4520-1648-1 (sc)

Library of Congress Control Number: 2010906450

Printed in the United States of America
Bloomington, Indiana

This book is printed on acid-free paper.

Dedication

I dedicate this work to my wonderful, God-given family for their unyielding love, encouragement and holistic support during this endeavor and to my family, the body of Christ.

To my mother, Lorene : This book is especially dedicated to you for a lifetime of casting your vision for my life and for your timeless sacrifice and substance to see me achieve the best that God has for me.

To my children and grandchildren: Taydra, Damian, Tony, Gabby, Imanuel, Hallel, Hannah and my offspring to come: My prayer is that you will always seek to have a prosperous soul. I love you all so much.

To my sisters and brothers: Clara, Paulette, Loretta, Johnnie and Willie: Thank you for your prayers, support and for always being there.

Acknowledgements

Special thanks to *Pastors Gary and Maya Taylor* for your continued inspiration & support and the platform to teach the *Inner Healing* principles.

Special thanks to Bishop Mary Banks, Former Pastor and *Spiritual Mentor for seeing and supporting the call on my life.*

Regina Rogers, *Associate Editor*

Darla James, *Ghostwriter and Associate Editor*

Gabrielle Cash, *Typist/Graphics*

Reginald Tolbert, *Front and Back Cover Design*

SPECIAL THANKS

Special thanks to my friends, family and partners for your encouragement and financial support to Healing of the Heart Ministries!

A heart felt thanks to every person who had the courage to share their stories and testimonies in the hope of empowering others to let go of their secrets and be made whole.

Contents

Preface

OUR NATIONAL T.V. PROGRAMS AND news sources reported the story of a half-brother and sister who were living together as partners. They had parented four children, were adamant in their conviction of loving each other and therefore believed that nothing could be wrong with their relationship. During the same period, a father (as reported by *Court T.V.)* was on trial for impregnating his teenage daughter. This was all during the time when a high profile actress' body had been discovered and the dissemination of her estate was being debated. One of her T.V. clips sent a message to her mother alluding that she (the actress) had been raped at the hands of another family member. More recently we sat in "awe" as we heard the recount of a father locking his daughter in his cellar for many years, fathering several children with her, while her mother lived above in the home never knowing. My book, Holes in the Soul, will share real stories of others, possibly your sister, your best girlfriend, your teacher, minister and others from every walk of life who, too, have the secret of incest or sexual abuse in their past.

Holes in the Soul will reveal and expose many truths about incestuous and sexual abuse. Incestuous abuse is real and it is not something that started in the new millennium. As a matter of fact, according to the Word of God, it began thousands of years ago.

Sexual abuse is an epidemic in our society. If we don't address the sexual abuse – *from a secular as well as spiritual perspective* – we will perpetuate a society of mentally and emotionally damaged adults who are dysfunctional in their relationships at home, work, church and in society at large, leading to a continuous cycle of broken lives.

In this day and time we will no doubt see more and more blatant appeals for the right to love and have intercourse with whomever one chooses, even if it is a family member. You see, where there is no God-given and morally sound vision, people will cast off all restraint. This means that they willingly operate in a "no controls, no checks, and everything goes" type of mentality. When there is no restraint, standards and protocols are also absent. With the revolution of technology and cyberspace and the few laws to govern them, we will continue to see and read about more perverse declarations and demonstrations of various sexual perversions, and deviation from society and our God given norms.

Healing of the Heart Ministries was specifically ordained and designed by God, for this time and season to expose the dark and hidden secret of incestuous and sexual abuse and ***to bring hope and healing*** to those who have suffered its consequences.

About the Author

Healing of the Heart Ministries, International was seeded in my spirit some 22 years ago in a church called **Bible Talk**, under the leadership and pastorate of Pastor Mary Branch. Pastor Branch is now the well-known and renowned Bishop Mary Banks of *Bible Teachers International.*

Dr. Banks was endowed with a gift of divine wisdom and revelation of God's Word. She taught us how to pray, study the Word of God and bring our lives under subjection to the Holy Spirit. It was Dr. Banks whom God used to not only speak prophetically the destiny that God had purposed for me, but also to give me the platform to allow the "seed of my calling" to germinate. From this ministry, Inner Healing was allowed to cleanse, purge and consecrate me, as well as to grow me up in the things of God.

And so it began some 22 years that God set in motion the first works of delivering and healing women who had been sexually and incestuously abused. Though I did not have the theological understanding of my calling at that time, it became clear to me much later that God had given me an assignment and anointing to bring *Inner Healing* to women who were hurting emotionally, mentally and physically and spiritually from incest and sexual abuse.

My first encounter with an incest situation was with a young woman who shared that her grandfather had raped her some years ago. She had married, but had not told her husband. The guilt and shame and fears that had shaped her perception of herself, along with the fear of rejection and other burdens of her secret were interfering with her ability to become pregnant. She and her husband wanted a baby, but she just couldn't get pregnant. That day God started the deliverance, healing, and restoration process in her life. We prayed, rebuked the enemy, and commanded every evil spirit, unclean and trespassing spirit to loose her mind and body in the name of Jesus. We spoke to her womb and declared that the "seed" of a child shall come forth. I felt led to tell her to share her secret with her husband; after all it was not her fault. Three months later she was pregnant with her first child.

I too, am also a survivor of sexual abuse; but it would be some 10 years after ministering in this area before I would realize that I had been sexually abused (in my case, inappropriately touched) for a period of time by one of my uncles. I will never forget how the Holy Spirit unlocked this part of my life and revealed it. The Holy Spirit revealed it to me while I was preaching. I was at the point of making the altar call for women who had been sexually abused by a father, brother, grandfather or uncle.

While talking, this "moving tape" reeled across my mind and I saw my uncle hold me up in the back room of our little house on 63rd Street when I was about 6 years old. The room was dark. It appeared as if no one else was in the house at this time. I saw my panties being pulled down and his fingers exploring my genitals. This happened on more than one occasion. I remember that it stopped when we moved to a larger house.

As you can see, I had totally repressed this situation, storing it in the hard drive of my brain. It was through the illumination and revelation of the Holy Spirit that I recalled the situation. As I thought back over my life, I tried to identify *the effects of the abuse* over my life. The one thing I immediately recalled was that I never liked for my body (no matter how shapely or thin) to be seen by my husband without clothing whenever we made love. I always wanted to make love in the dark. I never liked the light. This was obviously a "shame-based" attitude that I picked up as a result of my abuse at 6 years old.

I write this book by the inspiration of the Holy Spirit of God, based on 22 years of experience in ministering to women, and a few men, who have been incestuously abused. Any steps to recovery that I will offer will be based on my ministry experience and the Word of God and other credible references.

Throughout this book, you will read "real stories" of incestuous and sexual abuse. You will learn about the effects of the abuse and I will share with you the steps that need to be taken in the recovery process and the pathway for *Inner Healing for the Soul*.

Chapter 1

Incestuous Abuse

Incestuous abuse is REAL! This is a season and time in our society where this type of abuse must be exposed for the devastating demon that it is. We don't hear about it from the pulpit, or even from our family members because we don't really know how to address the issue. We were taught that our dirty laundry is ours and we don't share family business with anyone else, even if it is killing us slowly – physically, mentally, emotionally and spiritually.

Incestuous abuse is as fatal to the soul and incurable as cancer is to the body. If cancer is untreated and unattended, the diseased person will ultimately die. Before death in the physical body occurs, the deadly disease causes an "auto immune" effect in the body, in which the immune system <u>actually</u> shuts down and no longer gives the body the protection it needs.

As cancers attack and destroy the physical body, so does incestuous and sexual abuse. Sexual abuse destroys a person's soul and breaks his spirit. The effects are a "shutting down" of the expected safety, trust and protection from those who are supposed to be protecting us. Our sense of well being and soundness, and the ability to live a functional, productive, healthy emotional life is severely distorted. From a psychological perspective, Maslow's Hierarchy of Mankind's Basic Needs teaches that the foundation of life is the need for safety, security, food and shelter. When the perpetrator of sexual abuse is the primary caretaker or provider, the very basic needs of a child are threatened. Simultaneously, the seeds of a dysfunctional spirit, soul and body are planted, which later spring up in a person's life. This type of abuse often limits one's development of healthy relationships in all areas of life.

As you can see, the effects of incestuous abuse are psychological, emotional, social and spiritual.

But glory to God, your help is at hand! Holes in the Soul will document some critical factors necessary for the sexually abused to start the healing process. My primary goal is to provide spiritual and practical information so that survivors of incest and sexual abuse and those who may currently be victims may become whole. Each of us has an innate, God-given ability to be made emotionally well and successful regardless of the situations, circumstances or relational challenges in one's life or from one's past.

What is Incest?

Incestuous abuse is nothing more than rape by a family member or a close family friend. It does not discriminate nor does it have respect of persons. It literally touches the lives of the rich and the poor. It transcends race, ethnicity, class or nationality. It is propelled by lust, which is an unrestrained desire for self-gratification.

Those who rape are fathers, grandfathers, mothers, cousins, grandmothers, brothers, sisters, uncles, stepfathers, step-grandfathers, stepbrothers, close family friends, momma's boyfriend, daddy's girlfriend, pastors, priests, clergymen, teachers, babysitters and the next door neighbor. There are times when a person of the same sex perpetrates this abuse.

I know with surety that once this secret weapon and silent killer of darkness is exposed, many will become "victors" rather than "victims" and will be empowered to have fulfilling, healthy relationships.

Incest is a silent killer of one's soul. Every human being has a soul which consists of his mind, will and emotions. Rape by a family member or close family friend, or a stranger, changes a person's ability and desire to live a normal life. In these cases, there must be some kind of comprehensive intervention that overrides the pain of the past and enables one to be healed and restored from the devastating and destructive effects of the sexual abuse.

This book has three major objectives: 1) to expose this dark, hidden, shame-based act and to show that it has been, and still is, prevalent in families; 2) to share real life stories of abuse and its effect on the lives of the victims, and, most importantly; 3) *to show that one can be healed, delivered, restored and set free from the negative effects of sexual abuse and live a healthy and productive life.*

Recovery for the sexually abused is a process. It may take a very long time, depending on the length of the abuse, the abuser and the degree of the abuse, among other things. Because sexual abuse transcends the body, soul and the spirit of a person, the stages of recognition, self-confrontation and reconciliation must take place before the abused can experience recovery and wholeness.

Regardless of the length or type of sexual abuse, the healing process starts on the "inside" of the abused. The abuse is done to the body, but the "effects" of the abuse are the pain and the memory housed inwardly in the brain, which is the center of life for one's perceptions, belief and behaviors. Typically, the outward appearance of men and women who have been and are being sexually abused looks like any other man or woman, boy or girl.

You see, incestuous abuse isn't anything we talk about or share with others; it is our *secret* and we keep it hidden, covered and neatly placed in our souls. Sexual abuse is oftentimes a life-long ache of pain, shame and guilt deeply buried on the inside. It is so painful that we "never" want to share the experience with anyone. Oftentimes, it is blocked, suppressed or repressed in the mind.

Our next chapter will reveal stories of those who found the courage to come out of hiding and seek healing from the pain of sexual abuse in their past.

Chapter 2

In the Words of a Survivor

AT THE TENDER AGE OF 14, I was shocked to find out that I was pregnant. You may say, "Oh you must have known," but no, this happened to me back in the 70's.

When the doctor announced that I was pregnant, my mother broke down and started to cry. I could not understand why she was crying. When we got home, she asked me how did I learn about sex and how to get pregnant? Still not understanding completely what she was saying, I innocently responded that I learned it from my daddy. You see, until this moment, I thought that everything in my life had been normal. My having sex with daddy was normal. That's how we showed our love for each other.

My mother called to my father and had me to repeat my response to how I had learned about sex. Once again, I responded that I had learned about sex from my daddy. When I repeated my response, he grabbed his heart as if he were having a heart attack. My mother beat me...that very day. From then on I knew something was terribly wrong.

I later came across a book about pregnancy. As I read the book, I realized what my father had been doing to me all those years. So at the age of 14, my whole life was shattered. I never knew that I was not supposed to have sex with my daddy. When I grew older and developed a relationship with the Lord, He revealed to me that the incest started when I was 3 years old...so it had simply been a **normal** part of my life. It was how daddy showed me he loved me; it was how I showed him I loved him.

Now, let me take you back to the things that were taking place...

- Not only did my father come to me in my room, I also remember one time when my mother, my father and I were laying in the bed together. My father lay between my mother and me. Though he was facing my mother, his hand was behind him while he was touching and fondling me. But you must understand that I thought this was a normal part of life.

- I remember times that Dad would come in the room, crawl in my bed and lay in my bed. Other times he would touch and feel me, even in the midst of us being at the dining room table, you know…a pat on the bottom, the breast…touching, kissing…you know. My mother was right there in the room.

- There would be times when Dad would come in the middle of the night and just snatch me out of bed, beat me, touch me, feel me, fondle me, strip me out of my clothes…and I never knew why.

My mother stayed sickly a lot, and now I understand that it was because of the pain and the hurt that she was experiencing. I really believe that my mother knew I was being sexually abused. She just blocked it out. Yea, she really blocked it out.

I now know that my father intentionally caused division between my mother and me. For example, if I did something wrong, mother may have told me that when daddy got home that she would have him to spank me. Well daddy would come in and take me in the bathroom and say, "I don't think that what she is saying to spank you for is worth it, so just pretend like I'm beating you".

I understand that he wanted to get my mind to a place where I couldn't trust mom...you couldn't tell momma nothing. And the biggest thing is the fact that it was just a normal life...a normal life. The people in our area would never have known that he was abusing me. When people came around, everything was normal.

Love was portrayed to me through the act of sex. That's how I understood love to be. When my father touched and felt and had sex with me in the bed...that's the way you loved. So if he would **not** touch me, or he did not feel or give me that type of attention...I would think that maybe I had done something wrong.

Sometimes I would go to him for that affection, because that meant he loved me. So if he wasn't showing me that love, it meant that something was wrong.

Chapter 3

A Man's Real Life Story

MY FIRST RECOLLECTION OF PERSONALLY knowing someone who was an "out of the closet" homosexual was a male relative. Though my family never verbally admitted it, it was obvious by his overt feminine mannerisms that he was truly struggling with his sexual identity. As a family, we were in denial.

During one period, I recall when he started to date a young lady and we were all so happy and finally breathed a sigh of relief that he was not gay after all. I had never heard of bi-sexuality or the "down-low" during those days. As time progressed, we had to accept the fact that our relative was a homosexual. Some of my family members chose to stay in denial and others in non-acceptance of his choice of sexual preference.

What we learned as time passed was that the root of his sexual preference was sexual abuse. As a young boy in elementary school, a man in the community who knew our family well had sexually abused him. This sexual abuse continued for a season of time. One day, I finally had the opportunity to talk openly with him regarding his homosexual lifestyle in the hopes of "converting" him to Christianity and "changing" his sexual preference. It was during this discussion that I learned of the sexual abuse that led him to enjoy that way of sexual pleasure and preference. His story is no different than what my studies and experience in working with women who are survivors of sexual abuse experience. The <u>seed</u> of sexual perversion (sexual addiction, promiscuity, homosexuality and lesbianism) oftentimes enters at the time of sexual abuse.

Other paths taken by the victims and survivors are compulsive behaviors such as drug and alcohol addictions, pornography, prostitution, compulsive eating and shopping and perfectionalism.

Chapter 4
The Story of a 45 Year Old Woman

I WAS INCESTUOUSLY ABUSED BY MY older brother from about the age of 6 years old until the age of 14. My brother was twelve years older than me. I remember one occasion when I was at his home after he had gotten married. While sleeping in the bed with his daughter who was 3 or 4 years old at the time, my brother got out of the bed with his wife and came into the bedroom where his daughter and I were sleeping and raped me in the same bed. I was scared; I cried! He said that he would not hurt me and he would not do it again. I was scared! I didn't have anyone who I could share this with because my family had put a label on me of being "fast." Each time my brother said he would never do it again, he did, at least twice or so a month.

I couldn't go to my father because I believe my father would have killed my brother, so even though I was abused, I was also afraid for my brother. I now know that I was protecting my brother. My family would not have believed me anyway. My brother rode a motorcycle, and there would be times when my mom sent us to the store and he would stop and take me into the grass to molest me. Mostly the molestation went on at his house whenever we had an opportunity to be alone. It happened for 8 years. When I turned 14 years old, I got my period. When I told him, it stopped because he did not want to get me pregnant. It never happened again.

At 16, I started sleeping with my elementary school instructor until I left for college at 18 years old. At college, I started to sleep around with boys and realized during my sophomore year that I was promiscuous. I continued in a state of promiscuity until I got married in 1981. I had given my life to the Lord in 1981, joined the church and was an active member. In 1981, when I got married, it was because I was tired of living that kind of life. However, my husband was perverted. He was bisexual! I was married for ten years.

During this time, I started going to a prophetic and deliverance church. It was there that God started to deliver me from my *past* and my *pain*. I became passionate about

God, and His Word. I came to realize that I could have a better life; a life free of rejection, anger, betrayal, hurt and pain. My husband was fifteen years older than I was; therefore, he controlled me even though I knew his lifestyle. Through the Word of God and the love of God, I realized that I could be free of man's control, domination and manipulation in my life. I learned that I am a new creation in Christ and that God has a better plan for my life.

My deliverance, healing and restoration came when I fell in love with Jesus, was filled with the Holy Spirit and my mind was transformed and renewed by the Word of God. I can truly say to every woman, man and child that God can deliver, heal and set you free from every hurt of your past. It doesn't matter where you have been, what you have done and how long you did it. Jesus' blood has made total provision for your restoration and wholeness. *Be ye healed in Jesus' Name!*

Chapter 5

The Story of a Female Incest Survivor

MY SISTER AND I WERE little girls when my brother began to molest us. Though for a long time, I couldn't recall the details because I was so young. Bits and pieces would come to my mind. Over time, I have been able to see what happened to us. I remember my sister and I had twin beds and slept in the same room. My mother worked at night. My older brother, who was in his late teens, babysat us when my mom was at work. Once momma went to work and we went to bed, my brother would come into our room and take turns molesting us. It started with getting in the bed with me and touching me in my private part.

As the Holy Spirit took me back to this situation, I could actually smell my brother's skin, and feel his flesh upon my flesh; though I don't recall that he ever penetrated me (that part I totally blocked out) I could actually smell his cologne and the odor of his body years later.

After my brother would get out of my bed with me, he would go to my sister's bed and do the same thing to her. We were only 5 and 6 years old at the time. As I can best recall, this went on for about a year. When we were around the age of 13 and 14, we told our mother, but she didn't believe us.

Because I was in church most of my life, I was hearing the Word and growing up in the things of God. However, I had a lot of sexual partners during my young life and now know that the sexual abuse was the contributing reason.

My road to recovery was through the power of God working in my life. I grew to love Him, and wanted to please Him. So I tried to live a life pleasing in His sight, which meant He had to purify me from the inside out. I have spent most of my adult life allowing Him to purge and purify my life.

I was not comfortable around my brother for many years because I had not confronted him about the sexual abuse. I thought I was okay. I wasn't! I finally got up the nerve to call my brother because I did not want to take our "distant" relationship into another year. Also, I knew I needed to confront this part of my past and release him. I knew I had to forgive him. Needless to say, his first reaction was to deny it. I expected that! I still told him what he did, how it affected my life and that I forgave him. I realized that forgiving him was for me and in obedience to God, my heavenly Father.

Chapter 6

The Story of Abuse at the Hand of a Cousin

I COME FROM A WELL-KNOWN AND respected family. My mom and dad had lots of sisters and brothers who are active in church, in the community and many were in college. My cousins and I always played together. We would oftentimes spend the night over at each other's homes on weekends. I recall that I was about ten years old and one of my cousins was about sixteen. Usually around 10:00 p.m., after we watched television, ate popcorn or candied apples or whatever treat my auntie had for us, she would make us go to bed.

All the bedrooms were upstairs and two of us would usually share a bed. My older first cousin touched my private parts when we watched TV or in the kitchen or upstairs when no one was looking. It was always quick and though I felt that it was wrong, he was one of my favorite cousins. He always bought us ice cream or popsicles from the ice cream truck that came around in the community. I thought nothing much about it until one Saturday night, my auntie made us go to bed early because we had to get up and go to Sunday school the next day. I remember being awakened out of sound sleep in the middle of the night and being carried downstairs. My cousin was carrying me. He whispered in my ear, "Be quiet; don't say anything." So I didn't. He took me into the closet downstairs, which was dark and had lots of stuff in it. It was crowded and smelly and dark. My cousin started putting his mouth on my mouth. Then he put his mouth on my private parts. We stayed in the closet for what seemed like hours. All the time, my cousin was kissing me all over my body.

That night was the beginning of every opportunity we found to be alone whether in the closet, bathroom, in my auntie's car, but mostly on Saturday night in the downstairs closet when everyone else in the house was asleep. My cousin would give me money and so I always had money for candy, ice cream, snow cones, and other things I wanted. As time progressed, my cousin started to put his private part up to my mouth and tell me to kiss it. I started to kiss it and my body felt good. My cousin would make strange sounds like grunting and "ah' and we would both be wet.

I wasn't doing well in school. My mother and I were not getting along. She was very strict. I really loved my father. He and I were close, but he worked a lot, so I preferred to be anywhere other than at home.

One day, when I was playing in our yard, my dad's friend who lived across the street called me over to his house. He was older than my daddy, but always came over to the house when daddy was home. They would sometimes have a beer on the week-end. When he called, "Come here", I went. I was about fourteen years old at the time. He told me he had something for me in the house so I walked in with him. He gave me money. I took it. He then started touching me all over and putting his mouth on me. I never told mama or daddy. I started to feel bad about myself. I knew what was happening to me was wrong. I knew what I was doing was wrong. I felt shame and guilt, but I didn't stop.

I graduated from high school and married the first guy who asked me, with whom I was already sexually active. We divorced a couple of years later. I was depressed and didn't like my life at all. I was drawn to men who offered me nothing but sex. I thought sex was love and I needed to be loved. I started abusing drugs in order to cope. I became dependent on them to numb the void and emptiness inside.

Having grown up in church, I was in and out but never finding peace. Things just stayed the same. I would spend the next twenty years of my life in and out of bad relationships and doing drugs to forget the pain of my past. A few years ago, I had a real encounter with God through Jesus Christ. Jesus told me that He loved me. That began my hope in getting emotionally healed and living a life of hope and inner peace. I now rest in the grace of our Lord Jesus Christ, knowing that He is my healer.

Chapter 7

Gee's Story

I WAS TEN YEARS OLD WHEN my stepfather started molesting me. My mother worked until late evening, which left the two of us together until she came home. My stepfather was kind to me and playful and I was oftentimes more comfortable with him than with my mother. As an adult, I now know that he subliminally molested me first and then moved on to the sexual acts.

One day when we were all alone, he said to me, "I need to teach you some things that you need to know." Then he proceeded to masturbate in front of me. When he ejaculated, he said, "Now look at this, this is what I need to show you, this is what it's all about." What it was all about is now being defined as incest.

During the course of the next four years, I would be subjected to a progression of sexual abuse. I recall walking home from school on a cold winter's day in my long coat and my boots with my books in my arms when he met me at the door with, "Now I'm going to show you what it feels like to be a woman." With that he wrestled me to the floor and performed oral sex on me right there in my pile of books, boots and all. It was just a short time after that he playfully wrestled me onto the couch and took my virginity. I was so mixed up and so messed up I didn't want to think or feel anything. Yet I could not escape the feelings of horror and disbelief, deception and betrayal, violation and disgust.

My stepfather had told me that he loved me and that he was looking out for me. I wanted someone to love me. I only spent two years with my real father; good years for me, bad years for my mother, and she never missed a chance to spew out hateful remarks about how she couldn't stand me because I looked just like or acted just like my father. Sometimes my stepfather would slip me money and would whisper, "Here, your mother doesn't want me to give you this, but I'm going to give it to you anyway." I began to hate him and her.

I tried to stay away from home as much and as long as I could, but yet it still happened again and again. One time, my stepfather carried me up the stairs to their bedroom and penetrated me right there on my mother's bed. He later told me that he caught a glimpse of the most horrified look on my face and that he could not bring himself to do it again.

Though he never raped me again, as a result of the sexual abuse, my life became painfully unbearable. I was so depressed that I did not want to get out of bed. I was dysfunctional, sexually promiscuous, and self-destructive. I equated sex with love, and since I needed to be loved, I loved sex. I hated my life and I hated myself.

I had been in church most of my life, but at the age of 24, I really started to seek God as my Lord and Savior. I wanted to love Him and be loved by Him. I knew that He could heal me and restore me. My process of healing began with knowing that even though I had been so angry, even with God, He still loved me. I was forgiven as long as I was willing to forgive. He became the person to whom I could go and share my secrets, my pain and all my thoughts. I began to trust Him more and more. The more I spent time with Him the more I wanted to be in His presence. As I learned more of Him and followed Him, my vision of myself started to change. I began to feel loved and worthy of love and accepted by God.

Over time, and after a process of many years, the love of God has healed many of my emotional scars, mended my broken heart, and is daily making me whole in Him.

I encourage you to draw close to God and He will draw close to you. Seek Him and you will find Him. Knock and the door will be opened. Ask and you shall receive of His abundant life for you.

Chapter 8

I Will No Longer Keep My Secret

I HAVE A SECRET! I AM going to share my secret with you because I do not want anyone else to have to keep a secret such as mine. The reality of my secret is that I kept it for such a long time, that it almost destroyed my life. I survived being sexually abused as a child. It may appear easy for me to say this, but it still hurts very, very deeply. I am sure you are wondering why I am so willing to share what happened to me with you. It is simple – because I care.

I was first molested when I was 3 or 4 years old. My first memory is of my aunt covering my head with covers when my perpetrator was changing his clothes. My thought at that time was she really did not have to do that because I had already seen "that." Now remember I was not older than 4 years old and I had such an adult thought. The molestation began with fondling, went to petting at about age 7, and on to intercourse when I was about 12 or 13. I was physically molested on a continuous basis at least once a month, until I graduated from high school. He continued to say vulgar things to me even while I was in college, until I finally threatened to report him.

You are probably thinking that I should have been able to stop the abuse when I got older, but my spirit had been broken and destroyed by that time. I cannot begin to tell you about the horror I lived on a daily basis. I remember one time hiding from him in a closet with a knife in my hand. I was around 12 years old at the time. I know that if he had found me, I could have killed him that day. The funny thing is, I never wanted to verbalize that feeling because I always thought it was evil of me to want to kill another human being. I had days when I was in my early teens that I actually missed days of school because I was "sick" because I thought I was pregnant. I was constantly afraid that I would become pregnant and then everyone would know what I had been doing.

I lived in a total world of fantasy. I made things up to make me feel better. I was never who I really was. Now, I know that sounds crazy, but the truth is, I was not living, I was simply pretending. Can you imagine waking up every day and having to pretend to be somebody because you honestly did not know who you were? My self-esteem was horrible and I always second-guessed myself. I did not date when I was in high school. I had lots of male friends, but that was it. I would let guys say whatever they wanted to me. As an adult, I have had one failed relationship after another because of the abuse in my past. I continued to choose to date the wrong people and found it difficult to be true to myself; so of course, I did not allow the men in my life to know who I really was. It was not until I started to realize that I was worth something and gave up trying to find someone to make me complete, that I finally ended up with someone who loves me because I am me – the good, the bad, and the ugly. This did not happen overnight. It took years to come to this point.

I can honestly say that from the time the abuse began until about 1997, everyone and everything else were more important to me than I was to myself. The fact of the matter is that it is still a struggle for me to put myself first. I have to constantly remind myself that I am worthy.

So, again, why is it that I am sharing all of this? The first issue I need to make you aware of is that MANY people knew what was happening to me. I found out later that family members, neighbors, and friends somehow knew and no one, I mean no one, attempted to help me. I will be honest and say that that has been one of the hardest things about the abuse. Everyone was afraid to help me. One of the explanations I received was that they did not want to upset my mom. WHAT ABOUT ME??? I was dying a slow death and no one cared. I actually thought it was just people around me who never helped children who were in the situation I was in, but that isn't true. I currently work as a Sex Offender Specialist Probation Officer. I hear the same story over and over again about how adults knew what the offenders were doing and they looked away. I also see the family members who refuse to believe the child and say they still trust the offender. Men who are actually court ordered to be supervised when around children are left alone with children because adults believe him over the child. This mentality allows perpetrators to continue to molest other children. As a community, we need to make it our business to rescue children who cannot rescue themselves.

There are so many people who just look the other way because they do not want to involve themselves in someone else's business. Well, guess what? IT IS EVERYONE'S BUSINESS IF A CHILD IS BEING RAPED OR MOLESTED? Not only did my perpetrator violate me, but all of the people who knew and remained silent violated me as well. How was I supposed to feel when I found out all of these people knew. People seem to be more comfortable reporting animal cruelty than child cruelty. Something is gravely wrong with that.

The other reason I am sharing my secret is because I want children who are being molested and adults who were molested to tell someone. We cannot continue to let all of the ugly feelings we have about who we are and what happened to us fester. If you are a child, you need to tell someone and keep telling someone until someone helps. I also know that part of keeping your secret is because you love the perpetrator and you do not want to hurt him or her. I know this because that is exactly how I felt. I was afraid <u>for</u> my perpetrator. I felt like he could not make it in prison and it would be all my fault. I did not want to hurt him like that. Even when I was angry with him for what he did, I did not want to hurt him like that; however, the truth is he had given me a life sentence and I did not even consider that. If you are an adult, know that there are people you can talk to. You can start with calling your local Rape Crisis Center, or talking to your pastor, minister or a counselor. Do something!

And finally, to those of you who are molesting children, there is help for you as well. You need to seek it immediately. You cannot continue to rob children of their spirits and think that it is okay. It does not matter if you "only" fondle the child or you are having sexual intercourse with them, you are robbing them of the essence of their lives. What you are doing is a heinous crime which, when caught you will not be looked upon fondly by the criminal justice system.

Those of you who are choosing to look the other way are an accessory to this unspeakable crime.

I am now on the road to recovery. It has been a long road indeed and one that I will continue to travel. I will always feel the sense of loss of what happened to me, but I now know that I can be whole again. I have learned through much soul searching and prayer that God wants me to tell my story. Perhaps in telling my story, I can do for someone what no one did for me. My intention is to tell my story to everyone I can because as long as I keep it a secret, I can help no one, not even myself.

If you know someone who you think may be being molested, please report it. If you do not feel comfortable to that child's parents, report it to the local child welfare agency. It is your moral obligation to rescue that child. You do not even have to tell them your name. Again, if you are being molested or have been molested, IT *IS* NOT YOUR FAULT AND *WAS* NOT YOUR FAULT.

I survived being molested and I hope that I have encouraged you to not keep secrets about sexual abuse, because those secrets kill your soul (mind, will and emotions) and your future joy, peace and righteousness in God.

Chapter 9

Incest is Not New

OLD AND NEW TESTAMENT BIBLE REFERENCES

THE WORD OF GOD CLEARLY shows that the sin of incest dates back to the Old Testament. Incest is impure, perverted sexual intercourse and sexual activity between family members and close family friends.

One account of biblical incest and **God's command** concerning such behavior is recorded in the 20th chapter of the book of Leviticus. The scripture declares that family members should not have sexual intercourse with other family members.

The following verses are excerpts from the 20th chapter of Leviticus, verses 11-21:

And the man that lieth (carnally) with his father's wife hath uncovered his father's nakedness; both of them shall surely be put to death; their blood shall be upon them.

And if a man lies with his daughter-in-law, both of them shall surely be put to death; they have wrought confusion; their blood shall be upon them.

And if a man takes a wife and her mother, it is wickedness; they shall be burnt with fire.

And if a man shall take his sister, his father's daughter, or his mother's daughter, and see her nakedness and she see his nakedness, it is wicked.

And thou shalt not uncover the nakedness of thy mother's sister, nor of thy father's sister for he uncoverth his near kin: they shall bear their iniquity.

And if a man shall lie with his uncle's wife, he hath uncovered his uncle's nakedness; they shall bear their sin; they shall die childless.

And if a man shall take his brother's wife, it is an unclean thing.

God goes on to say in verses 23 and 26:

"Ye shall not walk in the manners of the nation which I cast out before you for they committed all these things and

I abhorred them…And ye shall be holy unto me: for I the Lord am holy, and have severed you from other people, that ye should be mine."

LOT'S DAUGHTERS

Contrary to God's commandments concerning sexual activity between family members, in Genesis19:31 we see that Lot's daughters got him drunk and each had sexual intercourse with him in order to conceive children because they feared that after his death they would not have anyone to carry on their race.

Verse 32 of Genesis 19 records Lot's older daughter encouraging the younger with the following words, "Come, let us make our father drunk with wine, and we will lie with him, so that we may preserve our offspring (our race) through our father."

Both daughters conceived a son by their father. If you notice, even back at that time, the daughters had to get their father, Lot, drunk with wine in order to sleep with him. The Bible clearly indicates that Lot was not aware of the sexual relationship his daughters had with him, because he had been completely inebriated. Here's the question that immediately springs to mind: "If Lot's daughters thought such sexual activity were legal, why would they go to such deceptive (excess use of alcohol) lengths to have sexual intercourse with their father?" Why not just share their concerns with their father and have intercourse while he was completely aware? It is clear that the daughters were aware of the immorality of their acts.

AMNON'S INCESTUOUS ABUSE OF HIS HALF-SISTER TAMAR

In 2 Samuel 13:2, we see that Amnon was vexed with a perverted sexual desire for his sister Tamar. The scriptures record that Tamar was a virgin and Amnon struggled internally with his sexual desires for her. The text says *"...for she was a virgin and Amnon thought it hard for him to do anything to her."*

Unfortunately, Amnon gave in to his immoral desires and schemed a plan to force (rape) his sister into a sexual relationship with him. He pretended to be sick and asked for Tamar to be the one who cared for him while he was on his sick bed. Tamar, being obedient to her father's command and completely unsuspecting of Amnon's scheme, brought food to her brother to help him recover from his feigned sickness.

This particular act of incest (rape and sexual abuse) between King David's son Amnon and Tamar, King David's daughter, is the beginning of the demise of King David's family and the death of two of his sons. As the story goes Amnon and Tamar were half brother and sister. They had the same father, but different mothers. Tamar and Absalom had the same father, King David.

Amnon ,the half brother, had a strong love (desire) for his half sister Tamar, whom the Word refers to as fair, pretty, lovely, attractive and good-looking. Amnon, with the help of Jon-a-deb, a scheming and conniving uncle, developed a plan for Amnon to be alone with Tamar for the purpose of raping her. The Word of God says he lay down in bed, made himself sick and sent for King David to come.

While there he asked the King if Tamar, his sister, could come and make him a couple of cakes in his sight that he may eat at her hand. Tamar, being obedient to her father, did as told. Here the plot thickens. The story goes on to say that when she brought the cakes in to where he lay, he asked her to come lay with him. She said, "No my brother, do not force me, for no such thing ought to be done in Israel". Howbeit, he would not hearken to her voice, and being stronger than she, forced her and had intercourse with her.

When we study the account of this incestuous encounter, we see so many "effects of the abuse" and the toxic emotional impact it has on a person in a single chapter of scripture. Some of the evil fruit (effects) produced from this scheme of the devil were:

- Ungodly counsel
- Craftiness, shrewdness and a conniving spirit
- Deception
- Lying
- Lust
- Force
- Folly
- Rape, incest, fornication
- Shame
- Violation of purity and innocence
- Lasciviousness
- Hatred
- Bitterness
- Betrayal
- Rejection
- Murder
- Depression
- Isolation
- Desolation
- Hopelessness
- Bareness
- Strife

- Covering/concealing/protecting/disguising sin. We typically cover sin with material things or money, for example.

While these particular examples occurred millennia ago, the effects of sexual and incestuous abuse remain the same and impact the lives of its victims generationally.

New Testament Bible References

In the New Testament, we see in I Corinthians 5:1 that Paul writes to the church of Corinth and refers to sexual intercourse between a step son and step mother as sexual immorality of the worst kind, an impurity of a sort that is condemned and does not occur even among the heathen; for a man to have his own father's wife (Amplified Bible).

The evil effects produced from sexual abuse are numerous, devastating and deadly to a person's spirit, soul and body. The psychological effects are far-reaching and can transcend and transfer from one generation to another. The Bible contains prohibitions of sexual relations between various family members and a number of states have severe laws to punish or avenge perpetrators involved in incestuous relationships.

Chapter 10

Consequences of Incest and Rape

WHEN A PART OF OUR body gets bruised, it becomes sore, tender, and dysfunctional. The composition of the tissue and cells change. We don't want anyone to touch us in that bruised spot because it hurts too much. Bruises don't always readily appear; particularly those bruises that have hurt on an emotional level. Though bruises are not always visible to the natural eye, the eyes of the soul are forever looking upon them.

There are many emotional "bruises" caused as a result of incestuous abuse. This list touches on some of them:

- Fear
- Guilt
- Shame
- Anger

- Bitterness
- Hatred
- Remorse
- Self-disgust
- Embarrassment
- Regret
- Disgrace
- Degradation
- Lesbianism/Homosexuality
- Prostitution
- Addictions (alcohol, drugs, sex, pornography, masturbation)
- Eating Disorders
- Perfectionism
- Compulsiveness Obsessive Behaviors (shopping, gambling, etc.)
- Offense (fall from grace, stray from the straight and narrow)
- Displeasure
- Insult
- Wounds
- Disgust
- Anger
- Madness
- Annoyance
- Vexation

- Irritation
- Aggravation
- Sin
- Error
- Transgression

The emotional pain brought on by incest and rape and other abuses is astounding, oftentimes going beyond imagination or understanding. How does a father or grandfather rape his own flesh and blood? We don't understand that; however, as evident in the stories we read, it is real and, perhaps more closely related to you than you realize. If not you, perhaps your mother, sister, auntie. What about your best girlfriend, your cousin, your boss? What about your husband, boyfriend, father or pastor?

Given the devastating impact, is there any wonder why some of the following social disorders and statistics are plaguing the church, meaning the Body of Christ:

- Over 50% of our marriages end in divorce
- Over 50% of the African American population is overweight
- Teenagers commit suicide at an alarming rate
- A woman is being battered every 5 seconds
- Christian homosexuality is on the rise

- 26% of children are raised in a single parent environment
- More revelations of clergy molesting children
- Alcohol, drugs and nicotine are destroying lives at an alarming rate
- 1 in 4 girls are being sexually abused
- Only 1 in 5 boys will graduate from college
- 1 in 6 boys are being sexually abused
- Potentially 80% of sexually abused people become lesbians, homosexuals, prostitutes, or sexual addicts

The consequences of incestuous abuse affect every area of one's life and causes dysfunctionality in every arena of life as we see above. In our interactive *Inner Healing for the Soul* workbook, I will address the more toxic emotions such as anger, bitterness, betrayal and others, in the hope that many will confront and work through their feelings and emotions associated with the pain of sexual abuse.

Inner Healing For the Soul

Interactive Workbook

PASTORAL ENDORSEMENT

Oh, to be awakened by the healing power of God! It is with tremendous *"Amens"* that I endorse this written work of Dr. Betty Mitchell.

Dr. Betty is an anointed vessel of God that offers comprehensive insight on the subject of healing our emotions. Through the "Inner Healing" classes she teaches at our ministry, many lives have been transformed.

As you read, study, and apply the living words of this manual and workbook, I invite you to experience the life of God-given liberty and joy. What an awesome journey awaits you in the pages of this work!

Pastor Maya Taylor
Open Word Christian Ministries,
Fairburn, Georgia.

INNER HEALING TESTIMONIALS

When the Inner Healing class was announced, I thought, "There are so many hurting people in the Body of Christ that need Inner Healing", so I prayed, "Spirit of the living God, order the steps of all who need healing in their body, their spirit and above all, their soul. Holy Spirit, meet them right where they are and arrest them. Go deep and penetrate their unconsciousness; heal, deliver and set them free, in Jesus' Name. Amen." I did not realize that a simple prayer for others would transform my life forever and draw me to a closer, deeper and richer relationship with God.

At this time I was feeling quite pleased with my Christian self. I was confident and I was in my God-ordained place (Open Word Christian Ministries). The Word was faithfully taught with simplicity and understanding and I was seeing *tangible results. I financially supported the work of the ministry. I rose early in the morning, committing personal time to prayer and the study of God's Word. I surrounded myself with godly and anointed friends who were Christ-focused and who challenged me to develop a closer walk with the Lord. I was living out my faith within the walls of corporate America on a job that I absolutely loved.*

Who would think I was hurting? I wore fine clothes, my make-up was flawless and I had a killer smile. I walked through tough times with poise and ease. I knew to put on the whole armor of God and fight the good fight of faith. My outward appearance was intact, but God saw my inward parts and He wanted to get to the heart of the matter. On the surface I looked great, but I was hurting deep down on the inside.

In the beginning, I attended the Inner Healing class to help Minister Betty set up the room, hand out materials and pray for others. However, by the third session, I was moved by the Holy Spirit and the Word of God that told me to listen, receive and be made whole! I thought, "Be made whole, aren't I in a good place"? Yes I was, but God had a better place. I felt God drawing my attention off of others and onto me. From that moment on, Inner Healing became very personal; the spotlight was now on my soul. The omniscient God (the all-knowing One) knew exactly where I hurt and why! I wish I could say it was easy and painless, and that I was suddenly healed, but it was and still is a process. I was reminded that before gold is purified and made ready to be used in unlimited ways, it has to go through the fire.

God was moving me beyond the seen to the unseen and it was all about me. Out of the billions of people on the earth, He wanted to spend time with me; He wanted to heal me. So, I made time to be alone with Him. Many nights, as if I were watching a movie of the years gone by, I saw myself as a little girl playing in the school yard…laughing and singing; then the painful memories started coming back. I remembered being called ugly and nappy headed. I saw myself in the car of a trusted family friend reading a book… then I had the memory of my breast being fondled. I saw myself as a teenage girl, awe struck by a boy for the very first time…then I had the memory of being teased and ridiculed by his mother. I saw myself in college, preparing to graduate and being excited about becoming an executive for a major retail chain…then I had the memory of my professor telling me that I'd never be successful in retail because I was timid, weak and unprepared.

Finally, after graduating from college without my Dad being in attendance, I had the painful memory of his death at age 50 from a heart attack.

Wow! I had all of these suppressed and painful memories that no one, not even I could see. Still, as I watched the movie of my life by way of the Holy Spirit, I saw patterns and behaviors. My understanding was illuminated. I began to say, "Oh that's why I said; I saw; I acted; I touched"! It all made sense! That's WHY! **In the midst of Inner Healing, I saw that I was carrying the weight of rejection, unforgiveness, anger, guilt and shame.**

I cried for days. I cried out to God from the depths of my soul. I wanted to know who, what, where, why, when? How could all this STUFF be in me? The answer to all those questions was summed up in a few words from Father God to me…"I am Jehovah Raphe, the Lord your Healer!"

At that point I stopped asking questions, I surrendered and I died! When I died to my way of thinking, and when I died to my will and my emotions, the healing process began! The next few months were amazing! I cried, laughed, talked (out loud), praised, worshiped, studied and fasted as I gently fell madly in love with Him Who knew me best…Jehovah Elohim, my Eternal Creator! I thank God for Inner Healing and I give GOD the glory that in my apartment, now my sanctuary, HE healed ME! I could go on and on and on as the Lord continues to mold, shape and LOVE me unconditionally into a gentler, kinder and more compassionate daughter.

Inner Healing has brought me to a place of love, peace and joy in the Lord that I never imagined possible. I no longer make time for God, HE is time. When He shows me something in me that's not like Him, I no longer ponder or ask who, what, when, where, why or how. I quickly repent, pray and move on up a little higher. My days are built around His agenda and daily I pray, "Lord, don't let me miss the assignment that You woke me up to complete today. Don't let me, my or I get in the way of Your perfect plan!"

Then with the anticipation of a little child in an ice cream store, I expect to taste and see the goodness of the Lord all the days of my life.

-Kathy Ervin

The Inner Healing message has helped me release emotional baggage from past hurts. I am now able to quickly identify and recognize negative suggestions (attacks) from the enemy.

I know how to take authority over it, cast down imaginations, and speak the Word over the situation. I am more confident in my faith and focused in my Christian walk.

I believe that Inner Healing is a continuous process of renewing the mind and confessing God's Word. I have just completed my second class! I chose to continue studying this subject so that I would be able to share with others. I highly recommend the Inner Healing to everyone.

Sharron Dickens Stradford

Chapter 11

Human Sexuality –
A Wonderful God-given Gift

"And the Lord God said, It is not good that the man should be alone; I will make him a help meet for him."

Genesis 2:18

"Therefore shall a man leave his father and his mother, and shall cleave unto his wife: and they shall be one flesh. And they were both naked, the man and his wife, and were not ashamed."

Genesis 2:24, 25

GOD'S ORIGINAL PLAN WAS FOR sex to be enjoyed within a marital relationship between a male and a female. Sex was given for God's covenant purpose of procreation of righteous seed and the other healthy pleasures that come with godly sexuality.

Our society is OBSESSED with SEX and HUMAN SEXUALITY.

In verse 21 of Genesis 2, we see that God caused a deep sleep to fall upon Adam, and he slept; and He (God) took one of his ribs and closed up the flesh instead thereof. With the rib, which the Lord God had taken from man, made He a woman, and brought her unto the man.

In *Genesis 1:27*, God had already made male and female, when He made man. *So God created man in his own image, in the image of God created he him: MALE AND FEMALE CREATED HE THEM.*

Genesis 1:28 says: *And God blessed them and said unto them,* <u>be fruitful</u>, <u>multiply</u>, *and* <u>replenish the earth</u>, *and* <u>subdue it</u>; <u>have dominion</u> *over the fish of the sea, and over the fowl of the air, and over every living thing that moves upon the earth.* When the serpent entered the scene in *Genesis 3*, he brought along deception, shame, guilt, a sense of nakedness, separation, and every form of sin and wickedness. This wickedness included sexual immorality.

Galatians 5:19-21 lists some of the works of the flesh:

- Adultery
- Fornication

- Uncleanness
- Lasciviousness
- Idolatry
- Witchcraft
- Hatred
- Variance
- Emulations
- Wrath
- Strife
- Seditions
- Heresies
- Envyings
- Murders
- Drunkenness
- Revelings

SEXUAL SINS

Sexual abuse, incest, sexual perversions and addictions are running rampant in our society. Sexuality is a multi-billion dollar industry via television, computers, movies, books, hand-held devices, etc. Children are stolen, sold and used as sex slaves. Fathers, grandfathers, uncles and stepfathers rape their sons, daughters, grandchildren, nieces and nephews at an unprecedented rate while our society appears to become more tolerant of such acts.

One in four girls is sexually abused before the age of 18; while one in 6 boys is sexually abused by the age of 18. Sexual abuse leads to compulsive and destructive behaviors such as:

- Bestiality
- Compulsive desire for material things
- Desolation
- Drug and alcohol abuse
- Eating disorders
- Group sex
- Homosexuality
- Isolation
- Lesbianism
- Masturbation
- Perfectionism
- Pornography
- Prostitution
- Self-hatred
- Sexual addiction

One of the most devastating assaults on a person is sexual abuse. It totally destroys a person's body, soul and spirit. Sexual abuse entraps one in a lifetime web of dysfunction and emotional pain.

Please take a look at the following list of some of the most common sexual sins facing the 21st century. Identify the ones you participated in as a child, teenager, and/or adult, whether by consent or by force.

The following exercise will help you to personally confront your past actions, take responsibility for them, and break the guilt, shame, power and control they have over you. Prayer and meditation on God's Word will help you to walk in total victory! However, professional counseling may be needed.

Please check all that pertain to you and meditate on each one.

If this exercise becomes too painful – STOP! Don't do it. In this case, you may need to meet with a Spiritual Advisor or Counselor.

Adultery

Bestiality (sex with animals)

Desiring to have sex with children

Excessive sexual fantasies

Fornication

Homosexual activities

Lesbian activities

Masturbation

Needing to have sex more than once per day

Sex in occult and/or rituals

Sex with best friend's girlfriend or boyfriend

Sex with clergy (ministers, pastors, deacons, etc.)

Sex with multiple partners at the same time

Sex with relatives and/or close family friends

Sexual activity that caused you to have one or more abortions

Sexual activity that caused you to want to commit suicide

PRAY THIS PRAYER...

God, You have commanded me to present my body as a living sacrifice, holy and acceptable unto you. My body belongs to You because You purchased me through the blood of Jesus, who redeemed, rescued and bought me back from eternal separation from You. Empower me to present my body holy and acceptable to You. Father, in the name of Jesus, I ask you to bring to my memory (my conscious mind) every person who sexually abused me and every person with whom I had sexual relationship by consent or by force from my childhood to adulthood. Additionally Father, enable me to <u>confront</u> every sexual sin and addiction within me, in Jesus' name.

Make a list as the Holy Spirit reveals. Write the name of each person the Holy Spirit brings to your mind with whom you have had an ungodly sexual relationship.

_____

_____

_____

_____

_____

_____

_____

Go back to the previous section entitled ***Sexual Sins*** and identify the ones that have had a negative impact on your life. For example, is there guilt or shame from having an abortion? Are you covering or hiding the fact that you were sexually abused? Be honest with yourself. Remember that recognizing and confronting your issues are necessary steps to conquering them.

List the sexual sins that have had a negative impact on your life:

_____

_____

_____

_____

_____

_____

Pray the *Prayer for Breaking the Power of Sexual Sins and Soul Ties*. This is an area which may require pastoral or professional counseling. Please get the help that you need.

PRAYER FOR BREAKING THE POWER OF SEXUAL SINS AND SOUL TIES

Father God, I come to You in the name of Jesus with thanksgiving and praise in my heart for Your grace and mercy in my life.

According to Your Word in Hebrews 4:16, I can come fearlessly, confidently and boldly to the throne of grace that I may receive <u>mercy for my failures</u> *and find* <u>grace</u> *to help in good time for every need coming just when we need it.*

So Father, I come to the throne of grace and ask Your forgiveness for every sexual sin and sin of immorality in my life. Please forgive me for every act, deed, thought or fantasy; whether acted out in my body or in my mind.

Father, I ask You to purge and cleanse my conscious, subconscious mind and conscience mind of impure and perverted sexual desires. I renounce sexual sins and soul ties of my past; I break the power of sexual sin and perversion in my life and pull down every stronghold of impure sexual imagination, evil and sinful desire, unholy affections, thoughts and fantasies in Jesus' name.

Father, with the Word of God and by the Blood of Jesus, I ask You to go back into my past and break the sexual soul ties, the sexual seeds of unrighteousness in my mind, will and emotions, for every man and woman with whom I was sexually active from a child until this very moment. Please forgive me. I forgive myself and ask You to release me. I forgive and release them in the name of Jesus. Wash me in the water of your Word and cleanse me with the Blood of Jesus.

Fill me now with your Holy Spirit and with the fruit of your Spirit. Help me to operate in temperance, chasteness, holiness and righteousness in Jesus' name I pray…Amen.

Whom the Son sets free is free indeed. I am free. I am cleansed. I am redeemed by the Blood of the Lamb! Amen

BREAKING SEXUAL SINS AND SOUL TIES
PERSONAL REFLECTIONS

NOTES

_____

_____

_____

_____

_____

_____

_____

_____

THOUGHTS / DIRECTION FROM HOLY SPIRIT

_____

_____

_____

_____

_____

_____

_____

PERSONAL ACTION PLAN

_____

_____

_____

_____

_____

_____

_____

_____

Chapter 12

The Three Fold Cord: Fear, Shame and Guilt

"And if one prevail against him, two shall withstand him; and a threefold cord is not quickly broken."

Ecclesiastes 4:12

THIS TEXT IN ECCLESIASTES TALKS about the three-fold cord that is hard to be broken. The author uses the illustration of the binding of cords to create a pictorial representative. When winding two pieces of cord together, a stronger hold is created than if only one piece of cord is used; however, a two fold cord can still be more readily unwound than a cord of three that is twisted or braided together in a woven pattern. In order to "undo" such a cord, one must understand and carefully unwind the pattern according to the same fashion in which it was originally created, only moving in the opposite direction.

So it is with the three fold cord of fear, guilt and shame. The enemy, who is more subtle than any beast of the field (Genesis 3:1) has used these three emotional cords to bind the soul of man in an effort to inhibit his release and thus his reconciliation to God and man. But oh, how glad I am that the light of God's Word reveals the "pattern" of this three fold cord and thus allows the Holy Spirit to "unwind" it and free our souls forever!

Until we receive the knowledge of the truth, these negative emotions and "crippling of the soul" that come from incest and sexual abuse and from other forms of abuse create strong negative emotion of "guilt and shame." Likewise, there is also a strong sense of guilt and shame that comes from a person who may never have been sexually abused, but who chose to have an abortion, or one whose fiancé doesn't show up at the altar for the wedding and she never hears from him until years later.

Each of these scenarios carries strong, painful memories and negative emotions. However, I have found in having dealt with all of these types of situations that there is a devastating covert stigma associated with the person who has been incestuously or sexually abused. There appears to be a "church theology" that sexual sins are "worse" than other sins. In my opinion, there is this prevailing notion that if I drink alcohol or gamble, that is not quite as bad as committing adultery or fornication. This is simply not true. God hates all types and kinds of sin; however, He loves the sinner, which is why He made a way, through Jesus Christ, to make a divine exchange. That divine exchange is that He took our sin and gave us His righteousness. Therefore, whatever the sin, we can repent, renounce it and be forgiven, delivered, cleansed, healed, restored and made whole by Jesus Christ.

God has a greater three-fold cord! His three-fold cord is Love, Mercy and Grace. Genesis 3 clearly declares that after Adam and Even sinned and fear, shame and guilt manifested, God came on the scene and asked, "Adam, where are you?" God already knew the answer to the question, but He wanted Adam to "see" himself and allow God to weave a triple cord of Love, Mercy and Grace.

We don't have to experience fear, shame or guilt because these toxic emotions do not come from God. God has made provision for an eternal three-fold cord of Love, Mercy and Grace to be available to us as believers. Additionally, He has given us an open invitation to come boldly to the throne of Grace to obtain the grace to help in the time of every need for every situation. What an AWESOME God we serve!

Cherish and manifest daily God's threefold cord of *Love, Mercy and Grace.*

Chapter 13

Christ Has Provided for Our Inner Healing

*"But he was wounded for our transgressions, he was **bruised** for our iniquities..."*

Isaiah 53:5

ONE OF MY FAVORITE SONGS is *"It Was the Blood that Made the Difference at Calvary."* Oh the blood of Jesus! Jesus was pierced in His sides by the Roman soldiers. Blood and water poured from Him onto the earth to redeem (rescue, buy back, deliver) us from eternal separation and damnation from God. The work on the Cross was to give us eternal life with God and to enable and empower us to manifest God's righteousness, His way of doing, acting and being in the earth. The blood represented redemption while the water represented cleansing. One of the things I believe we miss in this scripture is the *bruised side of the cross:* the bruises and the blood that remained on the inside of our Savior for our Inner Healing and wholeness.

Furthermore, Isaiah 53:5 says that He was wounded and crushed for our sins. He was beaten that we might have peace. He was whipped, and we were healed. The Life Recovery Bible gives an account that Jesus was beaten that we might have peace. The King James Version of Isaiah 53:5 states that He was *"bruised for our iniquities."*

THE BRUISED SIDE OF THE CROSS

As you begin the Inner Healing process, you must consider t*he bruised side of the cross. Jesus was the Perfect Sacrifice:*

- Jesus was wounded for our transgressions
- He was bruised for our iniquities
  - When one is *bruised*, blood is formed on the inside and settles on the inner layer of the <u>skin</u>.
  - A *bruise* is a discoloration, mark, an injury, a mar, wound, hurt or damage.
  - *Iniquity* is defined as the inner sins that are hidden or housed in the heart (inside); they can be covered or disguised.

-Certain triggers will expose iniquities of the heart.

- *Iniquity* ,as defined in the New Testament, is "anomia" and it means "lawlessness" and "wickedness", which indicates a violation of God's law.

• Jesus was our chastisement and by His stripes were healed – Spirit, Soul and Body

Like a bruise, hurt and pain from our childhood are kept in the <u>unconscious</u> part of our brain. The unconscious part of the brain is referred to as the *limbic* or *old brain*. The old brain records the feelings and memories associated with pain, hurt, abuse, rejection, abandonment or offense at the time it occurs.

A NATURAL EXAMPLE OF BEING BRUISED...

I recall coming in from church one evening and while walking up the stairs I twisted my foot. Later, as I prepared for bed, I realized that my foot felt a bit uncomfortable, so I inadvertently looked at the bottom of that particular foot. I noticed that the blood had settled right below the surface of the foot and manifested as a large, dark discoloration. The blood did not break through; rather, it settled on the inside of my foot. The Holy Spirit used this natural example to demonstrate that Jesus too was bruised on the inside for our inner hurts and pain, our brokenness of spirit, soul, heart and body.

It is God's desire that we live an abundant life. God wants us to have a life that is full and overflowing with peace, joy and righteousness. It is His desire that we are whole (meaning nothing missing or broken) and that we are free from the cares, agitations and burdens of the world.

It is God's desire that we become emotionally healthy and successful as we grow and learn of Him as well as realize and accept who we are in Christ.

To get back to the original state of wholeness and prosperity of spirit, soul and body, we must allow the Holy Spirit go inwardly to *root out* everything in our soul realm (mind, will, emotions) that entered and/or affected us during our formative years. We must allow the Holy Spirit to gently reveal every image, thought, secret, every memory and to illuminate within us all that is not of Him.

The Holy Spirit is the only One who can lay the axe to the *toxic roots and fruits* of our life, dig out the pain, hurts and darkness, and then plant love, joy, peace, righteousness and wholeness.

Jesus declares in the scriptures, *The thief cometh not, but for to steal, and to kill, and to destroy: I am come that they might have life, and that they might have it more abundantly. (John 10:10).*

Many Christians and non-Christians are deeply wounded and are being destroyed by toxic emotions in their soul.

The very *core* of the Inner Healing is to get to the root of offenses, hurts, abuse and pain within your soul, which causes toxic emotions, ungodly character and promotes unhealthy and dysfunctional behaviors, actions and deeds. Before we live an abundant life in Christ, we must first pull down, throw down and root out every emotional and mental stronghold within ourselves.

Mental strongholds are the beliefs and attitudes we formed as a result of experiences from birth to adulthood. A *stronghold* is a belief system, a fortified thought, image, fantasy or philosophy.

The brain, like a computer chip, stores every experience whether good or bad. Those experiences shape our personalities, temperament, character and belief systems. In order for the soul (mind, will, and emotions) to come into harmony and balance with the Spirit, we must allow the Spirit of God and the Word of God to transform, change and renew our mind, according to *Romans 12:2*: *And be not conformed to this world: but be ye transformed by the renewing of your mind, that ye may prove what is that good, and acceptable, and perfect, will of God.*

Thank God for Jesus who was bruised for our emotional health. Jesus was the perfect Sacrificial Lamb who took away our sins, tore down every wall of partition and provided for our Inner Healing and emotional health. Oh, the Blood of Jesus!

Chapter 14

The Process from Abuse to Wholeness

"And the very God of Peace sanctify you wholly; And I pray God your whole spirit and soul and body be preserved blameless unto the coming of our Lord Jesus Christ."
I Thessalonians 5:23

"Faithful is He that calleth you, <u>who also will do it.</u>"
I Thessalonians 5:24

IN PREVIOUS CHAPTERS WE HAVE established that incestuous and sexual abuse are real in our society, our families and churches. Reportedly, one in four girls and one in six boys are sexually abused before the age of 18. We have also shown that sexual, especially incestuous abuse is dark, secretive, hidden, concealed and covered by most victims and/or survivors for a period of time as evidenced in the true stories documented in the book. In addition to the stories presented, we also relayed bible stories to further support that incestuous abuse is as old as the bible. We have also documented some of the "effects" from the devastating acts of sexual abuse such as betrayal, bitterness, shame, guilt, anger and so on, as well as, some of the behaviors that are outputs of sexual abuse.

At this point, we are going to transition into the process from deliverance and healing to restoration and ultimately wholeness. According to I Thessalonians 5:23, God wishes that we be made whole. The word "whole" (kalil) in the Old Testament means entire, perfect, all (meaning to the fullest extent). In spite of and regardless to what the situations and circumstances of our lives have been, or are, God wants us to be whole (entire: perfect and without blemish). Whole (hygianion, hygies) in the New Testament means "to be sound", healthy, well, safe and sound; it also means "restored" and "healed". From the very beginning, God wanted man and woman to be whole and to live an abundant life (to the full extent and overflowing) with His provision of joy, peace, and righteousness. However, sin entered through craftiness and deception, producing shame, guilt and a separation from the abundant life God prepared for us. God then enacted another plan to redeem (buy back, rescue, deliver) man back from sin's eternal separation from Him.

Before we go forth into the steps to wholeness, it is important that I define and give you an understanding of the differences in "healing", "deliverance", and "wholeness". It is possible to get delivered or healed and not be made whole. God wants us made whole as indicated once again in I Thessalonians 23: "And the peace of God sanctify you wholly, and I pray your whole spirit, soul and body be preserved blameless unto the coming of our Lord Jesus Christ. Wholeness is being filled with the <u>fullness</u> of God's heart, mind, personality and nature. It is being mature (perfect) in Christ to a point where "forgiveness" comes easy; where offense and abuse no longer hold you in bondage, captivity and enslavement. It is a place we come to where the love of God and the grace of God abide in our hearts constantly for the sole purpose of fulfilling the plans and purpose of the life God predestined and prearranged for us.

Chapter 15

Healing

"...and as many as touched were made perfectly whole."
Matthew 14:36

MANKIND IS MADE IN THE image of God. We are made spirit, with a soul and body. According to the Word of God, because of sin in the land, and in our mortal bodies, we need healing for our bodies, our soul and our human spirit. God in his sovereignty and foreknowledge provided in the plan of salvation every provision we would need for the healing of soul, body and spirit. Isaiah 53 declares that we are healed. Most times when we think of healing, we think of healing for physical ailments or disorders like heart disease, diabetes, high blood pressure and mental disease. However, God's heart and mind for us is healing in our minds, will and emotions as well.

Emotional healing and health are important to God because He specifically declares in III John 1:2 that we are His beloved, and as so, He says I wish above all things that you prosper and be in <u>good</u> <u>health</u> even as you soul (mind, will, emotions) prospers.

The word "healed" in Greek is translated rapeuō which is the principal sense of "cure". Cure means to restore to health; make well, eradicate sickness from; to remedy or correct.

The Hebrew word for healer is rāphā meaning "physician"; Jehovah Rāphā, meaning "the great physician", not only heals physical conditions, but He also heals our emotional disorders and diseases, our broken hearts and broken spirits. He wants to personally renew our body, soul and spirit.

I am particularly adding this chapter to encourage you to receive God's emotional healing just as you would His physical healing, and to go <u>beyond</u> healing to wholeness, which will be discussed in another chapter. You see, many people get <u>delivered</u> from the <u>behaviors</u> associated with emotional pain, but don't become whole in Christ.

When I speak of getting healed, or delivered, and not being made whole (complete, entire, consecrated, totally at peace with God, others and yourself) I must have you look at behaviors. A behavior is an action or an operation, emanating from inwardly or within, in the form of one's conduct, attitude, acts, deeds, practices or habits. Therefore, it is possible to get healed (have the pain eradicated or stopped) without ever dealing with what caused the pain in the first place. I call this going back to the "root" cause. In order to get whole, we must go back to the root (what caused the pain) and allow the "root cause" to be fully recognized, processed and addressed according to God's instructions.

In the physical, an example would be much like going to a medical doctor because you are having severe pain in your chest. The doctor may give you medicine to heal (eradicate the pain; cure the pain); however, if he does not know where the pain came from, it will come back again. Though the medicine caused the chest pains to go away, the "root cause" of the pain is still dormant in your body. If the doctor does not perform additional tests, analysis and diagnostic procedures to determine what caused the chest pain in the first place, it will manifest again in the future. You see, what the doctor dealt with was the symptoms. He medicated the symptom. Though the chest pain is eradicated, for the moment, you may later get a little numbness in your hands, toes, a little tightness in your chest, dizziness in your head or your equilibrium may be off at times because only the symptoms were medicated or attended to.

Until the doctor determines what caused the chest pain, symptoms will continue to come. However, once he determines the root cause and "cure" the causal, then the <u>symptoms</u> will stop. So it is in the physical, it is in the spiritual; therefore, when we have been sexually abused and emotionally scarred in so many areas of our lives, healing may just deal with the symptoms, not the root. We learn to exist and to tolerate the symptoms because oftentimes the root is blocked, blacked out, buried, suppressed, or repressed.

When we are healed or delivered, but not whole (complete, entire, sound, well, in full emotional health),we will continue to manifest toxic emotions and behaviors.

In the next section, we will take a look at emotional health, for which God has made abundant provision.

EMOTIONAL HEALTH

Emotional Health is having peace. For the believer, it means having no questions, doubts, unbelief or concern for what others think about who you are in Christ. In a state of emotional health, the believer knows God's purpose for his life. It is a sense of total peace about your past, shortcomings, mistakes you have made in your life.

Emotions are a part of our soul (mind, will and emotions) and were meant by God to be good. In the book of Genesis, after God breathed His life (zoē) into Adam, He and Adam were in perfect alignment and fellowship. His original intent for mankind was to live a life of joy, peace, and righteousness by simply obeying His instructions. Wholeness was inherent in God's original plan for us.

Adam was in a perfect environment, with perfect surroundings and with perfect health, a perfect future and a perfect wife until he disobeyed the instructions from God. God's plan of obedience for our lives is for our protection. However, once sin entered the picture, what was once perfect, pure and chaste became defiled (dirty, soiled, stained, dishonored and disgraced) enabling our emotions to become damaged, debased, dis-eased and bruised; hearts become broken, minds became confused, undisciplined and held captive by another force or power; one's will becomes enslaved to another's will of the flesh rather than the will of God, our Father.

Most incestuous abuse takes place when one is a child, in some cases as early as infancy. A baby is chaste and pure and perfect as far as the sexual organs are concerned. I also believe that they are pure and chaste as far as their sexual orientation and preference are concerned, except in some extreme medical cases. Just as Adam was perfect, pure and consecrated unto God, and his wife Eve, before the fall, <u>so were you</u>. However, just as the enemy, a deceiver, a rapist, a controller, one full of ignorance and lust, and lifted up in pride, defiled the very existence of Adam and Eve's surroundings, environment and life, so was your entire"being" assaulted and defiled by someone who was supposed to love, protect, nourish, and provide all that was good for you. A child doesn't know right from wrong at that age; a child trusts almost everyone; they are easily enticed with candy, a toy, a smile, open arms, etc. Therefore, a part of the emotional wholeness process starts with your understanding that the abuse was not your fault. Even though Satan's plan was to kill, steal and to destroy you, God has a greater plan and that is to give you an abundant and prosperous and peaceable life - a life that is complete, entire, sound with nothing missing or broken.

Chapter 16

Deliverance

"From the LORD comes deliverance. May your blessing be on your people."

Psalms 3:8 (NIV)

ELIVERANCE IS A WONDERFUL BENEFIT of the redemptive plan of salvation; however, there is so much more that God has for you. Remember John 10:10 says that the enemy (Satan) comes to kill, steal and destroy, but Jesus (the Word) goes on to say, but I have come that you would have <u>life</u> more abundantly (full and overflowing). Deliverance stops the negative behaviors, praise God, but God, through the washing of the Holy Spirit wants to then purge, cleanse and sanctify the " one delivered" so that he or she will no longer be bound or enslaved to the past and the sinful nature that was dominating the soul prior to deliverance.

I recently met a young lady who went to the altar for prayer and was supernaturally delivered (set free) from drugs, alcohol, nicotine and sexual addictions. This young woman felt completely abandoned by her mother and father. As a child, the last time she saw her father was at the age of seven, even though after remarrying and starting a new family, he lived in the very same neighborhood as her. About three years ago, as an adult, she finally saw her father again and he tried to sell her drugs, further deepening the sense of abandonment and rejection she felt.

She was raised by her grandmother until the age of twelve, and then brought back to her mother's home, mostly to take care of her two younger brothers. Her mother lived in a neighborhood where drugs, crime and illicit sex were rampant. As a result of feeling unloved and abandoned, this young woman sought out love and fulfillment in sex and drugs. She became sexually active by the age of 11, was raped by her cousin at the age of 12. By the age of 23 she had been sexually active with over 18 people. This included acts of adultery, fornication and lesbianism. Not once in these sexual occurrences did she experience any pleasure or love.

Her involvement with drugs began around the age of 11 or 12 and quickly escalated from cigarettes and alcohol, to marijuana, cocaine and ecstasy.

Miraculously that day at the altar, in a "nanno second" she was made totally free by the power of God, and several months later has not had a desire for any of her previous imprisoning behaviors. Though she was set free from the strongholds on her life, her soul realm was filled with shame, guilt, anxiety, fear, abandonment issues and so on, as a result of her past.

It is absolutely essential for us to understand that in order to live the abundant life and to walk in the joy, peace and righteousness of the Holy Spirit, we must go to the next level after deliverance; which is cleansing, purging, restoration, wholeness in Christ Jesus the Anointed One, and total consecration to God, enabling a Spirit-led life.

Chapter 17

Steps to Being Set Free

"If the Son therefore shall make you free,
ye shall be free indeed."

John 8:36

THE BLOOD OF JESUS CHRIST has made provision for every situation and circumstance of our lives. For every snare of the devil, God has given us a way of escape. One of the benefits of our salvation is *Inner Healing.* Isaiah 53 declares what I call the bruised side of the cross meaning that God left blood (bruises) on the inside of Christ for our weary souls and our broken hearts. It was God's original plan that we be whole. He never changed his mind about that. Jesus Christ is our Inner Healer. If we are in Christ, His Spirit lives on the inside of us; therefore, God has given us the divine ability to exercise our will to allow the Holy Spirit to go within and totally restore us to wholeness.

I believe the reason we are hurting so much as believers is because we have not understood the anatomy of our pain. Neither have we gone to the origination (root) of our pain nor allowed the painful process of uprooting to take place. Rather, we make room for the secrets and pain and thereby ensure that they are comfortably housed inside our souls. We have allowed our past to define who we are, what we do, how much we accomplish, how we feel about ourselves and others, how long we live and the quality of our lives. In other words, we let the situations, circumstances and toxic relations win.

Beloved, the Word of God says we are victorious in Christ. We are **more than** conquerors in Christ Jesus. As adults and teens, we must deal with the pain, hurt, disappointment and unmet expectations of our past.

To begin the journey to freedom and wholeness from the bruises and brokenness within, there are some essential steps that must be taken:

1. Recognize that you have a problem. If one does not <u>see</u> that he has a problem, he will never take a step to fix the problem. He will continue in denial.

2. Admit that you have a problem – You must <u>admit</u> and own your problem. Begin the process of facing the realities of your past and your pain.

3. Stop blaming others – Human nature is to blame someone else for our behaviors and actions or plight in life. As far back as the Garden of Eden, we find Adam in Genesis 2, saying to God *"…it was that woman you gave me."* Adam blamed the woman and God. For it was God, he reminded Him, who gave me that woman in the first place. And in turn, the woman blamed the serpent. And so it is with us! If we can put the fault or blame on someone else, it takes it off of us. The abuse you experienced was not your fault, but *it is your life*. **Come on and take your life back!**

No matter who you are, what you are facing or what you have done, God wants to <u>break</u> the curse that is "in" you or "on" you. He also wants to reverse the pain and shame of your past and release "the blessing" in your life and the lives of your family members.

Remember, there is no bondage that God cannot reveal and then completely heal. He is the God who sees, knows and has already made provision for your wholeness through His son Jesus Christ. He looks deeply beyond the surface and sees the root cause for every area of weakness and pain we feel; seeing us clearly, Jehovah Rapha comes with healing and releases us to a life of hope and liberty.

Oftentimes when we think of mental health, we think of someone being "crazy"; or having lost their mind. This is a myth. Mental health pertains to the "soulish realm" of our lives and it affects both our "body man, our soul man and our spirit man".

When we speak of mental health issues, we are referring to things such as: fear, depression, anxiety attacks, addictions, anger, rage, food/eating disorders, diseases, infirmities, suicidal tendencies, etc. When we know and understand that God has come to heal us wholly and completely we are ready to move forward on our journey to wholeness.

God is tells the prophet Hosea, "My people are destroyed for a lack of knowledge (*no understanding of the Word of God*)" (Hosea 4:6 KJV). I believe that as a result of reading my book, *Holes in the Soul*, your knowledge of the devastating effects of incestuous abuse and rape, and the understanding of the power of God to break the strongholds of the past, will lead you out of destruction into a life of abundance and peace.

Additionally, I have written an interactive workbook entitled *"Inner Healing for the Soul"* which will enable you to identify the specific areas you would like or need deliverance or healing in. The workbook *"Inner Healing for the Soul"* is designed to allow you to work through toxic emotions like Anger, Rejection, Betrayal and other negative behaviors at your own pace and in the privacy of your inner court.

WHY INNER HEALING?

The word of God declares that it is not what is outside of a man that makes him unclean but rather what is on the inside of a man (Mark 7:15). Out of the abundance of the heart a man speaks (Matthew 12:34). It is what is inside that will come to the outside, guaranteed!

Before you can see a doctor you must complete a form that asks about your family's medical history – father, mother, grandparents, and siblings. They ask questions like: Is there any history of cancer, diabetes, heart disease, addictions, T.B., mental illnesses, etcetera? They ask these questions so that they can get to the **root** of your present condition, and help you avoid future health challenges. Doctors know that problems in the bloodline are the origin of most health problems. They understand that it all begins in the DNA. If the root of every health problem is located within the DNA, this is where we need to begin; in fact, it is where Jesus began when He gave His life for ours and shed His blood (DNA) for ours. To understand this, we need a paradigm shift. That is, we need to change the way we view our current circumstances and situations and lay hold to the biblical paradigm wherein Jesus reveals a whole new perspective, according to Romans 8:1,2 which states, *"There is therefore now no condemnation to them which are in Christ Jesus who walk not after the flesh but after the Spirit,"* and II Corinthians 5:17 which states, *"Therefore if any man be in Christ, he is a new creature: old things are passed away, behold, all things are become new."*

A PARADIGM SHIFT

Our new paradigm shift all begins in the DNA of a loving, Heavenly Father. We must change what we see in the natural to the spiritual.

Jesus shed His blood (DNA) in an exchange for ours on the cross of Calvary. We have access to the blood of Christ and thereby His DNA <u>through the Word of God</u>.

The iniquity of Adam had us sick – the Blood of Jesus (the 2nd Adam) made us whole.

In this new life in Christ, all things become new in every area of the soul realm: the mind, the will and the emotions. Let's get some clarity on exactly what the soul realm encompasses.

SOUL REALM

- <u>MIND</u>
  - Intellect
  - Cognition
  - Consciousness and Unconsciousness
  - Faculty as the seat of human reasoning and understanding
  - A person's innermost being
  - Human volition (decisions, free will, choices)
- <u>WILL</u>
  - One's wish
  - One's desires
  - One's wants/need
- <u>EMOTIONS</u> – feelings, affections, desires
  - E (up, out and away)
  - Motions- Movement passion, agitation, sentiment, zeal, vehemence, heat, warmth, love, hate, anger, jealousy, sorrow, sadness, despair, fervor

When Jesus comes into our heart, He makes all things new. He recreates our total being and empowers us through the Blood of Jesus and the Word of God to be healed from the inside out. He renews our very soul and begins a healing process from the inside out.

Chapter 18

The Key to a Prosperous Soul

"Now thanks be unto God, which always causeth us to triumph in Christ..."

II Corinthians 2:14

THE KEY TO VICTORY AND success in having a prosperous soul is acknowledging and accepting inner hurts, pain and abuse. Furthermore, you must allow the Holy Spirit (with love and gentleness) to walk you through a process of confronting each of those areas, owning them and casting them down upon Him. Even now at this very moment, the anointing of the Holy Spirit is available to heal every past and present hurt, offense and every form of abuse. Some pain is so deep and so painful that it will take time, and maybe even professional counseling to get from pain to healing to wholeness.

True prosperity is loving God, loving your fellowman and loving yourself (despite your imperfections). True prosperity is knowing and doing those things God brought you to this earth to do. It is about knowing and doing your purpose and fulfilling the plans He has for your life. True prosperity is operating in unconditional love and genuine forgiveness regardless of the wrongs done to you. True prosperity is a *dying to self* and a **total surrender to God**.

True prosperity is looking into the *cup* of hurts, pains, abuse, offenses, disappointments, discouragements and every evil deed or act done to you and saying, as Jesus said: *"Nevertheless Father, Your will be done in my life."* Once we come to that place and time of total submission and surrender to God of all we are and all we have, then we can (like Jesus) say, *"Nevertheless."* I believe that when Jesus looked into the cup, He saw every form of sin and abuse, deception, denial, darkness, and eternal separation from God. These things do separate us from God and each other. Then He looked and saw His purpose, destiny and the plan God had for Him as it related to mankind. He was sent to redeem us. At this point I believe that He said, *Nevertheless.*

If we are going to live a prosperous life in Christ, we must look beyond our pain, abuse and hurts to see the plan, purpose and destiny God has for our lives so that we may live the abundant life in Christ which is soul prosperity. If you are in need of coming to Christ as your personal Savior, I invite you to take a moment to come with me to Calvary and pray this prayer of faith:

"Heavenly Father, I come to you as a sinner in need of Your grace. I believe that Jesus Christ is the Son of God and that He died and shed His blood for my sins and rose again for my justification so that I would be in right standing with you. I receive Him by faith into my heart for my complete salvation, deliverance and healing. Thank you for forgiving me for all of my sins and receiving me as your child."

If you prayed this prayer, welcome to the family of God.

Beloved, the blood of Jesus has empowered you to prosper in your mind, will and emotions. The following selected chapters from the workbook, *Inner Healing for the Soul,* will be a guide to assist you on this journey to freedom in Christ. You will find that you will flow readily through some sections and other areas will take time and prayer. Just know that God's plan is to bring you into perfect healing in your body, mind and spirit. ***Go forth and be healed in Jesus' Name!*** Amen.

Chapter 19

Betrayal

"At that time many will turn away from the faith and will
betray and hate each other ..."
Matthew 24:10

ONE OF THE OUTCOMES OF incestuous abuse and rape is the spirit of betrayal. It is important that we fully understand the spirit of *betrayal* and the negative impact betrayal has in our soul realm.

Betrayal is defined as disloyalty, unfaithfulness, to sell out, inform against, to double cross, to deceive, to trick, or a breach of faith or commitment. The effects of betrayal will first manifest in the soul realm (mind, will and emotions), specifically, the emotional realm. The most immediate effect of the betrayal is the emotional impact on the person betrayed. The greater the trust you have in the people who betrayed you, the greater the impact the betrayal has on you; hence the greater the distress you will feel.

When someone has betrayed you, it is highly likely that you will not easily trust that person again. Trust is fragile and can be lost in an instant. When a person has been betrayed, they will want to seek justice (making it right, remuneration, amends, atonement, chastisement, etc.). When the act that caused the betrayal is a secret and one feels that there is no justice (making it right, atonement or amends), the person betrayed houses the hurt, pain, disappointment, guilt and shame in the emotional realm of the soul. Betrayal, if left unresolved, will feed the mind toxic thoughts, images, desires, and distort one's reality of trust and commitment.

Betrayal will cause one to lose his identity and take on a distorted and oftentimes toxic view of who he is. It will cause one to feel a myriad of emotions, as seen in the story of Amnon and Tamar in *II Samuel 13*. Look what happens after Amnon raped Tamar (his sister):

Tamar put ashes on her head and tore the ornamental robe she was wearing. She put her hand on her head and went away, weeping aloud as she went.

II Samuel 13:19

Prior to the incestuous rape by her brother, she wore the garment of a king's kid. This garment also represented her purity and chasteness. However, after her rape, her garment (her identity) was changed and she was as a common person. This incident sends her into isolation and desolation, which is a common characteristic of one who has been betrayed. Once you have been betrayed, trust, loyalty and faith have to be re-established toward the person who betrayed you.

Chapter 20

Bitterness

"Let all bitterness, and wrath, and anger, and clamour, and evil speaking, be put away from you, with all malice..."

Ephesians 4:31

I WAS RECENTLY BETRAYED BY A family member, and experienced firsthand, the strong negative fruits of bitterness. There is a strong desire for justice when one is betrayed. I thought, *"If only the person would just admit that he or she was wrong and is sorry for hurting me."* My flesh wanted to strike back, to retaliate, to vindicate myself, to ensure that real truth was known. I also wanted to distance myself from this person and cut off communications, support, etc. It was one of the greatest wars of my soul that I have ever experienced. It took weeks of prayer and seeking God's face for His grace to forgive, let it go and be reconciled.

Forgiveness is a choice. Forgiveness appears to be much harder when one perceives that an injustice has been done to him. I know from my own experiences. I wasn't ready to forgive. I was not wrong. I was not the one who needed to apologize or initiate forgiveness, or so my emotions told me. There were several times I went to the telephone to make that call (the person I needed to forgive lives in another state) and every time it was like a 300 pound gorilla was holding me down; however, I couldn't move forward with the book or in ministry in a state of unforgiveness. Several weeks later, by the grace of God, I picked up the telephone and made that call to start the process of reconciliation. Every step was painful, but I loved God more and wanted to please Him even more, in spite of my hurt, disappointment and emotional pain.

Feelings of hurt or abuse will trigger toxic emotions. Those toxic emotions will eventually control our thoughts and our will if we don't bring them under the control of the Holy Spirit and the Word of God. When our emotions are out of control, we experience feelings of rejection, betrayal and anger, among other negative emotions. We are more likely to cover the pain instead of deal with the pain. We allow the hurt to affect who we are, what we do, and the plans and purposes God has ordained for our lives. These emotions ultimately lead to a root called **BITTERNESS**.

The word *bitter (mar* or *marah)* means anguish and great distress, or sorrow. *Job 3:20* points directly to the soul (mind, will, emotions): *Wherefore is the light given to him that is in misery, and life unto the bitter in soul.* Verse 21 goes on to convey that the soul in bitterness longs for death, which indicates that a deep state of bitterness can lead to depression and suicide.

Which long for death, but it cometh not; and dig for it more than for hid treasures.

Job 3:21

Bitterness can consume you if you let it. It is a powerful negative emotion that can be provoked by grief, sorrow, jealousy, loss of deep relationships, anger and disillusionment.

When a root of bitterness sets up residence within the soul, everything you do, think and say will be filtered through that bitterness. Here are some of the fruits that manifest as a result of operating in bitterness:

- Iniquity
- Isolation
- Loss of Identity

- Jealousy
- Murder
- Pain
- Pride
- Resentment
- Unforgiveness
- Deception
- Depression
- Envy
- Harshness
- Hatred
- Hopelessness
- Anger
- Cruelty

These spirits lead to addictive and compulsive behaviors. They shape the way we see others and ourselves. They can become IDOLS in our lives.

The Scriptures speak to us about the spirit of bitterness. *Genesis 37* shows that Joseph's brothers allowed bitterness to grow into hatred and attempted murder. We also see in *Genesis 4:3-8* that Cain's anger turned into bitterness, hatred and murder.

The following scriptures also speak about bitterness:

Let all bitterness, and wrath, and anger, and clamor, and evil speaking, be put away from you, with all malice.

Ephesians 4:31

Looking diligently lest any man fail of the grace of God; lest any root of bitterness springing up trouble you, and thereby many be defiled.

Hebrews 12:15

Bitterness is caused by extreme or persistent hurt and/or abuse (misuse). A bitter person has most likely experienced betrayal, rejection, brokenness, extreme disappointment and abuse in many forms.

Pain in the body is an indication, or symptom, of a physical disorder. Most infirmities, diseases or maladies will be discovered due to a physical pain. When we have a physical pain in the heart, we immediately go to the hospital. In such a case, persons with heart problems are prioritized above everyone the doctor sees because a heart attack is an immediate threat to the life of the body. However, when we have a mind attack or an emotional attack in our soul, we do not take immediate action to ensure soul health and recovery.

We must realize that it is impossible for the body to be healthy while the mind is sick, weak and damaged. While we may be look like we have a healthy body, a sick mind is often covered, concealed and nicely tucked away in the subconscious part of our mind. Yet it affects our thoughts, images and behaviors. The truth of the matter is that everything about us will mirror the condition of our soul (mind, will and emotions). Therefore it is imperative that we take immediate care of the hurts and pains in our soul so that the root of bitterness can be uprooted by *forgiveness and love*.

BITTERNESS IS ON A MISSION

Bitterness wants to hold you captive and accomplish the following things in your life:

1. *Enslave you...*When you are a slave, you do what your master says. Bitterness wants to control and master you. What you fail to master will eventually master you. This master tells you to hate, be angry, walk in unforgiveness, and oftentimes to murder (as seen in the Scripture in *Genesis 4* and *Genesis 37*).

2. *Set up a spirit of iniquity...* Iniquity is sin in the heart, wickedness and lawlessness. It is designed by Satan to steal, kill and destroy your LOVE walk with others. Iniquity also

steals and destroys your faith. Faith worketh by LOVE.

3. ***Kill your spirit...***A broken spirit is void of joy, peace, gladness, contentment and godliness. *Proverbs 15:13* says that *a merry heart maketh a cheerful countenance; but by sorrow of the heart the spirit is broken.*

4. ***Paralyze your effectiveness in doing the work God has called you to do...***You murmur and complain that nothing or no one is right. You lose sense of purpose and vision. You don't feel like praying, fasting, reading the Word or meditating. You are blinded and consumed by your own hurt and pain. You judge every situation and circumstance out of your pain. Bitterness blocks the voice and/ or conviction of God.

5. ***Stop forgiveness...***Forgiveness is a commandment, not a choice. Forgiveness is sacred to God and critical to your deliverance and freedom from the oppressor. (See *Matthew 6*)

THE SPIRIT OF BITTERNESS EXERCISE

1. List some of the negative emotions you felt or feel against the people who hurt, offended or abused you in the past.

_____

_____

_____

_____

_____

_____

_____

2. How did you deal with <u>your</u> emotions? Did you talk about them or allow them to remain inward?

_____

_____

_____

_____

_____

_____

_____

3. Did you reconcile with the person(s) who hurt you?   Yes   No

    If your answer is no, be sure to read, *"Healing from Bitterness"* on the next page.

4. How did you handle the situation?

_____

_____

_____

_____

_____

_____

_____

_____

HEALING FROM BITTERNESS

The following keys are vital to your healing process:

1. **Admit that you are in pain and that you are bitter.** You may be depressed, suicidal and angry; or you may feel very lonely. Admit that you are powerless to change your situation.

2. **Find the root cause of the pain.** When did it start? Why did the pain start? Who caused the pain? Think back as far as you can so that you can get to the root cause of the pain.

Ask the Holy Spirit to give you revelation and illumination of the situation.

3. **Confess the pain or abuse to the Lord by praying this simple prayer:** Lord, lead me in the way of righteousness and the peace of God. Heal my hurts and my pain in the name of Jesus. I thank You for the blood of Jesus that heals and protects me from all of the hurts of my past. Heal me oh God and I shall be healed, in the name of Jesus!

4. **Forgive the persons responsible for your pain.** Yes, you must forgive the people who abused (misused) you. Build an altar right there where you are and talk to God about the people who hurt you. Release them to God. Ask God to forgive them and to give you the grace to walk in forgiveness. In the book of Job, the Word declares that when he prayed for his enemies, his captivity was turned.

5. **Forgive yourself.** There is no condemnation to those who are in Christ Jesus *(Romans 8:1)*. Start to see yourself as God sees you. Be sure to read the chapter, "Who You are in Christ," and the *"I Am"* confessions.

Purpose in your heart to be emotionally healed and God will do the rest.

PRAYER OF FORGIVENESS FOR THOSE WHO HURT YOU

Write the names of all the people who have offended you, hurt you, harshly judged you, falsely labeled you or in any way brought you feelings of emotional pain or distress.

Names:

_____

_____

_____

_____

_____

_____

_____

_____

Call each person's name when you say the following prayer:

Heavenly Father, I choose to forgive _____ right now of any offense committed against me, whether knowingly or unknowingly. I release to You all of the memories and toxic emotions of bitterness that have been buried in my heart. Allow Your blood to freely flow and forgive me as I forgive _____. I release this event, situation, or circumstance of offense against me to You right NOW in the name of Jesus. I declare that it is released forever. Father, I ask You to heal me like only You can. Please give me the grace to move forward in the freedom and strength of forgiveness that I can only get from You. I believe that I have received your grace to forgive _____ and I thank You for that right now in the name of Jesus!

BETRAYAL AND BITTERNESS
PERSONAL REFLECTIONS

NOTES

_____
_____
_____
_____
_____
_____
_____
_____

THOUGHTS / DIRECTION FROM HOLY SPIRIT

_____
_____
_____
_____
_____
_____
_____
_____

PERSONAL ACTION PLAN

_____

_____

_____

_____

_____

_____

_____

Chapter 21
The Spirit Of Offense

"A man's wisdom gives him patience; it is to his glory to overlook an offense."

Proverbs 19:11

AUTHOR JOHN BEVERE STATES IN his book, <u>The Bait of Satan</u>, that "...the greatest bait in the Body of Christ is the *spirit of offense.*" It is a bait (lure, trap) that the enemy uses to entrap us. The bait often attaches itself to the emotions, which are located in the soul realm. When emotions are wounded, scarred, or out of control (i.e., not at ease), then the bait will attach itself to the pain or the hurt within us.

Offense is defined as:

- A bringing about of one's downfall as a consequence of sin

- A trap to cause someone to sin
- A snare – pitfall, deception, trick, lure, bait or decoy
- A transgress – sin, evil deed, iniquity or wrongdoing
- A trespass – an unlawful entrance or invasion of a person's territory or property; to enter unlawfully, to intrude; an act of immorality
- A stumbling block
- A law breaker (outside of God's or man's law)
- A covenant-breaker, one who breaks a vow
- An insult – to treat rudely (discourteous; impolite; crude in behavior; harsh). The offense most visibly seen and the one most often committed which causes one to fight and/or flee.

The spirit of offense comes to stop the flow of love, unity and harmony. How can two walk together unless they agree? The mission of offense is to put us in disagreement and at odds with each other. This breaks the number one New Testament commandment, that we love one another.

One of the questions most frequently asked during the time of Inner Healing is – why are Christians so easily offended? Again, offense stops the flow of God's love and forgiveness. It causes strife, division, schisms and every evil work of Satan.

Satan wants the Body of Christ, local congregations, families and friends to be divided, <u>yet</u> a house divided cannot stand. As Christians, we must do everything possible to guard against being offended. Don't take the bait. The Word of God tells us in *Luke 17:1* that it is impossible for offense not to come; however, we don't have to receive the offense. When the fiery dart of offense comes at you, put up your shield of love, peace, joy, temperance, longsuffering, forbearance and forgiveness.

Let's look at seven keys that help to guard against receiving an offense.

SEVEN KEYS TO GUARD AGAINST RECEIVING AN OFFENSE

1. **Love one another.**

   We are to love God first and to love our neighbors as ourselves. (*Matthew 22:37-39*)
   For this is the love of God, that we keep His commandments. (*I John 5:3* – Obedience)
   A new commandment I give unto you, That ye love one another; as I have loved you (*John 13:34*)

2. **Know your purpose and your current assignment.**

There is passion in purpose. Passion ignites the peace of God, a rest in God, an insatiable fire to please God. Passion eliminates jealousy and envy. If your passion for God does not lead you to the heart and mind of God and the love of God, you will respond to offense with your flesh, or in a carnal way (according to the works of the flesh listed in *Galatians 5:16,17*), which is borne out of your old nature.

3. **Practice operating in the fruit of the Spirit.**

But the fruit of the Spirit is love, joy, peace, longsuffering, gentleness, goodness, faith, meekness, temperance: against such there is no law. (*Galatians 5:22,23*)

4. **Guard your heart.**

Keep thy heart with all diligence: for out of it are the issues of life. (*Proverbs 4:23*)

5. **Be swift to hear, slow to speak and slow to wrath.**

The tongue is a fire of iniquity. It defiles (soils, stains, makes dirty, dishonors, degrades) the entire body. (*James 1:19; 3:5,6*) However, the Word of God tells us that a "soft answer" turns away wrath. (*Proverbs 15:1*)

6. **Forgive quickly.**

Exhale all negative thoughts, feelings, images and suggestions. Forgive so that you may be forgiven. Always ask yourself what God would do in <u>every</u> situation. *Ephesians 4:13* admonishes us to be perfect (mature) and grow into the measure of the stature of Christ. Christ is full of love and righteousness and He <u>acts</u> accordingly. He has commanded us to, "*be ye holy for I am holy.*" For if ye forgive men their trespasses, your heavenly Father will also forgive you: But if ye forgive not men their trespasses, neither will your Father forgive your trespasses. (*Matthew 6:14,15*)

7. **Always ask yourself what God would do in every situation.**

Ephesians 4:13 admonishes us to be perfect (mature) and grow into the measure of the stature of Christ. Christ is full of love and righteousness and He acts accordingly. He has commanded us to, "*be holy for I am holy.*"

As Christians we must be willing to allow Christ to break every yoke, even the spirit of offense. We can begin by praying this prayer.

Father God, please forgive me for taking an offense. Your Word clearly admonishes me not to take an offense when they come. Father, I repent in the name of Jesus. Please give me the grace and mercy to put up a shield of love and faith to guard against offenses. It is in the matchless name of Jesus I pray. Amen!

Next, write a letter to God similar to the letter below asking God to empower you be able to deal with the spirit of offense whenever it comes.

Dear Jesus,

I am writing You today because I need Your help. I am easily offended – hurt, insulted, in emotional pain, in unforgiveness, depressed, in willful sin, or have been abused and/or have secret sin in my heart. Please enable and empower me to grow and develop into a mature Christian who combats offenses with love and forgiveness.

List the names of the people who have offended you:

1.

2.

3.

List the circumstances or situations that cause you to be easily offended:

1.

2.

3.

Finally, write your letter to God.

_____

_____

_____

_____

_____

_____

_____

Now pray:

Father, in the name of Jesus, I release these situations, circumstances and relationships to You and ask You to take them and the burden of carrying and covering them from me now. I put them under the blood of Jesus and declare my freedom and deliverance from them. Please forgive me for holding on to them and not forgiving and letting go in Jesus' name.

Thank You Father for hearing and answering my prayers in the name of Jesus, the Anointed One! AMEN!

THE SPIRIT OF OFFENSE
PERSONAL REFLECTIONS

NOTES

_____
_____
_____
_____
_____
_____
_____
_____

THOUGHTS / DIRECTION FROM HOLY SPIRIT

_____
_____
_____
_____
_____
_____
_____
_____

PERSONAL ACTION PLAN

_____
_____

_____

_____

_____

_____

_____

_____

Chapter 22

Abandonment

"...I will not fail you or abandon you."

Joshua 1:5

I HAD A DISCUSSION WITH A young lady prior to writing this chapter who disclosed a surprising revelation that the broken relationship with her father left her oftentimes feeling abandoned by him. What was even more revealing is that her feelings of abandonment from her earthly (biological) father cause her to sometimes feel that God has also abandoned her.

She went on to say that this strong feeling of abandonment causes her to shy away from God when she should be running to Him for answers, direction, praise, worship, fellowship and communion. Deep down in her soul realm, she feels that God (her heavenly Father) will treat her the same way that her earthly father treated her.

Her feelings about God are typical for those who have a broken, distant or non-existent relationship with their earthly father.

An earthly father should be the one who provides for you, protects you and ensures your safety and sense of well-being. He should help you to grow and develop into a healthy and wholesome citizen of society, and should also nourish the gifts, talents, and abilities God gave you. Most importantly, he is supposed to give you back to God. The above scenario experienced by the young lady with whom I spoke, is unfortunately the rule rather than the exception. Abandonment also occurs when one has been emotionally wounded, scarred or abused by a spouse, pastor or other figures of authority in one's life. To **abandon** means to desert, depart from, leave behind, withdraw from, quit, give up, jilt, cast aside, renounce or turn one's back on. Abandonment operates in many forms. For example:

- Someone leaves or gives up on a covenant relationship (such as in a divorce).
- A parent gives a child away to a relative or puts them up for adoption.
- Someone may be with you physically, but not emotionally available to you. That person

withdraws their affections from you, though they are still physically present.

- In sexually abusive situations, a child tells a parent that he is being sexually abused and the parent does not believe the child. That child begins to experience a strong feeling of parental abandonment.

A well-known TV evangelist has shared on national television a number of times that she was incestuously abused by her father for several years. She recently stated that she felt abandoned by her mother, who knew she was being abused but did not intervene. She also felt abandoned by her father who sexually abused her on a regular basis.

The seed of abandonment comes into the soul (mind, will, and emotions) when a father, stepfather, grandfather or guardian abuses someone who trusts them. These are the protectors and providers, the ones responsible for emotional well-being, physical safety and security of the children in their care.

Let's look at some statistics:

- One in four girls is raped by the time they are 18 years old.

Note: The father or stepfather is responsible for 11% of these rapes. The grandfather is responsible for a smaller percentage of these rapes.

- 29% of all forcible rapes occur before the victim is 11 years old.

Of the women to whom I have ministered over the years, the youngest age of rape by a father occurred at 3 years of age. A 3-year old is still a baby, in many cases, barely even potty trained. When these children become adults and learn about God, they begin to wonder why God abandoned them at the time of abuse. They ask questions like:

- Where was God when I was being sexually abused?
- Why didn't He protect me?
- Does God love me?
- Why would God allow this to happen to me?

When a person is abandoned <u>for any reason</u>, certain perceptions set up in his conscious and unconscious mind. These behaviors begin to shape his attitude, personality, self-image, self-esteem, self-worth and confidence.

One of the first steps to *Inner Healing* is the acknowledgment that you have an abandonment problem. The common *fruits and effects* of abandonment are listed here:

FRUIT	EFFECTS
Anger	Hostility, wrath, rage, fury, madness
Compulsive Behaviors	Threats, self-harm, harm to others, substance abuse, food addiction
Co-dependency	Enabling another in his/her weaknesses or destructive behaviors
Desolation	Not letting people get close to you; if they leave, you won't hurt so badly
Distance	Ruin, emptiness, sadness, barrenness, destruction, devastation
Fear	Oppression, anger, depression, obsession, suppression, repression, hopelessness, anxiety
Isolation	Disconnection, separation, seclusion, detachment, aloneness, loneliness
Loneliness	Feeling alone, even when people are around
Low self-worth/self-esteem/self-image	Lack of self-confidence, low regard for self, disrespect, insecurity, introversion

| Rejection | Dismissal, refusal, ridicule, looked down upon, disregarded |
| Performance Approval | People pleaser; work for approval |

Self-worth: how you <u>value</u> yourself

Self-esteem: how you <u>feel</u> about yourself

Self-image: how you <u>see</u> yourself

Performance approval or performance *perfection* (being a perfectionist) is a huge deal for people who have been abandoned. They work long and hard (like a workaholic) to ensure that they are approved and accepted by family, friends and co-workers. They feel that they can work or perform well enough so that people will stay with them rather than leave them.

All of these fruit of *abandonment* manifest when a person decides that the pain of someone leaving them is too great to experience again. Therefore they stay in an abusive situation to hold on to that person. This person's trust in others has been severely violated and it is difficult for them to trust anybody.

Furthermore, people who have been abandoned are likely to go into isolation. **Isolation** is a *defense* or *protective* mechanism. It is a place of retreat for self-protection, safety and security. Loneliness is an empty and unfulfilled place. We saw an example of isolation in the story of Amnon and Tamar (*II Samuel 13*). After Tamar's half-brother (Amnon) raped her, she retreated into a place of isolation and desolation, which was protected by deception, silence, bitterness, hatred and rage.

It is important to understand that the child who was abandoned (or perceives abandonment) will manifest the fruits of abandonment, as previously listed. Those behaviors need to be addressed and cured by mental health professionals, pastors, counselors or other qualified persons. In addition, always remember that God is sovereign and is able to supernaturally deliver and restore a person to wholeness.

If not dealt with, feelings of abandonment will continue to negate one's value, worth, self-esteem and image. So at the right time in life, the abandoned person needs to address the fears and issues of abandonment in order to have a healthy (but humble) self worth/value.

When we operate in a spirit of abandonment, the lenses that we see ourselves through are clouded by how we *feel* about ourselves from the **inside**. This is why *Inner Healing* is so critical to recovery. It is so important to look into the soul realm (mind, will, and emotions) to understand where the *child* is trapped, even though you are now an adult. You must understand the negative emotions associated with abandonment issues. In order to live a healthy emotional life, the *little girl* and the *little boy* must be confronted and healed.

If you are experiencing any of the toxic fruits of abandonment, you *must* take the following steps to start the recovery process:

1. Recognize and acknowledge that you have experienced or are experiencing abandonment issues, some of which are:

   - Anger
   - Co-dependency
   - Compulsive behaviors
   - Depression
   - Desolation
   - Fear
   - Feelings of emptiness inside
   - Insecurity
   - Introversion
   - Isolation
   - Loneliness
   - Low self-esteem/image
   - Perfectionist
   - Rejection

2. **Acknowledge you need help.** Write down what you are feeling and why. Try to remember when you first began to feel abandoned.

_____

_____

_____

_____

_____

_____

_____

3. **Get help!** The spirit of abandonment is a root with a lot of fruit! The help that you get must be specific to each individual situation and need. You may benefit from any of the following types of help: *pastoral counseling, professional counseling, self-help books, support group or counsel from your local clergy.*

Whatever you choose to do, please know that emotional healing, deliverance, and restoration of your soul is available through people, groups, mental health professionals, secular counselors and Christian counselors.

Let's take a look at key terms concerning self-esteem:

- *Self-esteem* has to do with how you *feel* about yourself. It has to do with whether you honor, respect, and regard yourself highly, as well as whether you demand respect and honor (of yourself) from others. It is feeling good about what you can do.

- *Self-image* is how you *see* or *look* at yourself and how you perceive the way that others *see* you. It is feeling good about who you are.

- *Self-value* is feeling good about the value and worth you bring to a situation or relationship.

Here are some things you can do to build or increase your self-esteem:

- See yourself the way God sees you
- Know who you are in Christ
- Answer the following questions:
  - What do you like most about yourself?
  - What do you like most about your body?
  - What would you change about yourself and why would you change these things?
  - What are your strengths?
  - What are your weaknesses?
- Tap into your own sense of humor (*it's in there!*)
- Meditate on the fact that God loves you

- Professional counseling
- Spiritual counseling
- A combination of professional and spiritual counseling
- Join a group with others who have experienced incest, rape, physical abuse, addictions or compulsive disorders

In closing, I pray that you honor the person you are and start to appreciate, accept, and love yourself – because God loves you. He sees you as fearfully and wonderfully made, created in His image and likeness!

I will praise thee; for I am fearfully and wonderfully made; marvelous are thy works and that my soul knoweth right well...

Psalm 139:4

ABANDONMENT
PERSONAL REFLECTIONS

NOTES

_____

_____

_____

_____

_____

_____

_____

_____

THOUGHTS / DIRECTION FROM HOLY SPIRIT

_____

_____

_____

_____

_____

_____

_____

_____

PERSONAL ACTION PLAN

_____

_____

_____

_____

_____

_____

_____

_____

Chapter 23

Fear

"For God has not given us the spirit of fear, but of power, and of love and of a sound mind."

II Timothy 1:7

FEAR IS ONE OF THE most-experienced and toxic negative emotions. Fear has the ability and capacity to torment and paralyze. *II Timothy 1:7* tells us that *God hasn't given us a spirit of fear.* This means that we can overcome fear and walk in total victory over this toxic emotion. So what is fear anyway? This is a distressing emotion aroused by impending danger, evil, pain, etc. Whether the threat is real or imagined, fear is the feeling or condition of being afraid. The following list contains examples of different people or things that may cause fear.

- Being alone
- Being in a crowd

- Being too hot or too cold
- Being physically attacked
- Claustrophobia
- Dad
- Darkness
- Death
- Dreams
- Failing Health
- Heights
- Losing someone you love
- Mom
- Not feeling safe/secure
- Not having enough food
- Not having enough money
- Siblings
- Step-parents
- Teachers

Because Satan is the master at making things appear to be something they are not, he uses fear to maintain his cords of fear, guilt and shame. He whispers in our ear that everyone knows our secret. He threatens that as soon as they find out who we really are, they will no longer love us. So with his trickery he tightens this three fold hold until we believe that there is no way out. We hide within the confines of these emotional barriers and simply exist. But today, is our day of jubilee. The alarm is being sounded to our souls. Jesus Christ has come to set the captive free; and whom He sets free, is free indeed! Break through the strong man of fear and walk in your power, love and soundness of mind. Walk in your freedom!

FEAR EXERCISE

1. List some specific people or things that have caused fear in your life. List everyone and everything that you can think of, whether you still experience that fear or not.

2. How did you handle your fear?

3. Do you still have any of the fears that you listed above? Yes No

4. List the fears that are still present.

_____

_____

_____

_____

_____

_____

_____

There are steps we can take to overcome fear and enjoy real freedom in Christ. Three steps to overcoming fear are:

1. **Identify the fear**. It is critical to pinpoint exactly <u>what</u> you fear and, if possible, <u>why</u> you fear it. Keep in mind that undefined fears immobilize us.

2. **Consider the worst thing that could happen**. I believe the worst thing that can happen is that the thing we fear will come upon us. Don't allow that to happen!

You have power over you fears. Mount up on your wings of courage, call your fears by name and command them to leave you; rebuke them in the name of Jesus and declare that fear is replaced with peace, courage, love, power and a well disciplined mind.

3. **Claim the truths of God's Word**. The truth will set you free (John 8:32). Read the following chapters pertaining to the will of God for your life:

- Psalm 27:1-3
- Psalm 46:1,2
- John 16:33
- Romans 8:31

Confess daily: *God has not given me a spirit of fear, but power, love and a sound (disciplined) mine. Amen!*

FEAR
PERSONAL REFLECTIONS

NOTES

_____

_____

_____

_____

_____

_____

_____

_____

THOUGHTS / DIRECTION FROM HOLY SPIRIT

_____

_____

_____

_____

_____

_____

_____

_____

PERSONAL ACTION PLAN

_____

_____

_____

_____

_____

_____

_____

_____

Chapter 24

Anger

"Be ye angry and sin not: let not the sun go down upon your wrath..."

Ephesians 4:26

ONE OF THE MOST DEADLY weapons in our society and families today is the spirit of anger. Anger is a negatively explosive emotion that can lead to hatred and murder if not timely and effectively addressed. The effects of anger in our society speak for itself. Simply listen to the news and it becomes crystal clear that we are living in a society where many men, women, boys and girls of all races are furious, enraged, filled with fear, despair and lack hope for a better life. Much of this anger is caused by deep childhood hurts and pain that have never been healed. Anger's <u>mission</u>

is to kill, steal, destroy, hurt or disconnect us from our fellowman whether it is a spouse, child, boss, clergy, etc.

WHAT IS ANGER?

Anger means to be hot, to heat or to boil. *'Aph* is the verb form of anger in the Old Testament. It means to breathe or snort. *'Aph* is thus nose, nostril or face.

Anger is a strong, negative, progressive emotion that emanates from the soul realm (mind, will, emotions) and can become very explosive and deadly. It is the general term for sudden violent displeasure accompanied by an impulse to retaliate. Its only mission is to avenge the persons who have hurt, offended, mistreated or abused. Anger can lead to hatred, physical, mental and emotional destruction, depression (heaviness) and murder if not brought under subjection to the Word of God and the laws of the land.

It is interesting to note that the Old Testament definition of anger alludes to the *breath* (from mouth), to snort (the nose) and the face. The face is formed with the gates of our body and the gates to the soul. Those five gates (also known as senses or faculties) are the eyes, nose, ears, mouth and hands. These gates serve the body and the human spirit of man until the Holy Spirit comes in at salvation and regenerates us to a new creation in Christ.

Therefore if any man be in Christ, he is a new creature, old things are passed away, behold, all things are become new.
                                                    II Corinthians 5:17

Prior to becoming a new creature, the five senses allowed sin (anger, wrath, fury, rage) to rule and reign in the mortal or human body (unregenerate soul). These five gates were servants to the body and our fleshy desires and appetites. Therefore, anger had free course to attack, lash out and avenge itself. Consequently, we appeased our anger the same way the unsaved appeased their anger. Like an entry in a computer, every time we become angry, an imprint is made in the brain and toxic chemicals are released into the body.

Let's look at different types of anger and how anger progresses...

1. **Hostility** – animosity, contention, fighting, conflict, battle, clash, dispute, bitterness, malice, argument or disagreement

2. **Wrath** – vexation, irritableness, indignation, resentment, hostility, animosity, displeasure

3. **Madness** - to be angry, furious, enraged, irate, incensed, crazy, demented, provoked

4. **Rage** – violent anger, wrath, extreme agitation, violent emotional state, madness, a storm, seethe, boil, continue violently, a <u>vehement uncontrolled anger</u>

5. **Fury** – unrestrained anger, frenzy, furor, wrath, ire (outrage, anger, indignation, resentment), outburst violence, fierceness, ferocity, intensity, severity, assault, attack, headlong rush. Fury describes deep and strong feelings aroused by injury or injustice. **Fury is a rage so great that it resembles insanity.**

The spirit of anger is progressive and explosive. If this emotion is not addressed through spiritual or professional counseling, it will boil over and take control of you.

II Samuel 13 gives an example of how anger led to death. Absalom had his brother killed for raping his sister Tamar.

For Absalom hated Amnon because he had forced his sister Tamar. Now Absalom had commanded his servants, saying, Mark ye now when Amnon's heart is merry with wine, and when I say unto you, Smite Amnon; then kill him, fear not: have not I commanded you? be courageous, and be valiant.

II Samuel 13:22, 28

Absalom's anger and hatred for his brother Amnon lay dormant within him for two years prior to having him killed (*II Samuel 13:23*).

Extreme anger may be blocked, blacked out, repressed or suppressed in the old brain (the unconscious area of the brain). Have you ever been around someone who is *mean spirited*, *quick tempered* or never pleasant to be around? It is highly possible that they have suppressed or repressed unrecognized anger as a result of offense or abuse.

Let me emphatically note here that anger will not go away by itself. If there is a spirit of anger or a stronghold of anger housed inside of you, ***YOU MUST GET HELP!*** The anger is looking for a way to *get out* or manifest itself. If not expressed, it will turn inward and cause depression or suicide.

The opposite of anger is love and peace with self and others. The Word of God tells us to live peaceably with all men (*Romans 12:18*). We are also exhorted to *be angry and sin not* (*Ephesians 4:26*). Furthermore, the Word of God tells us to *let all bitterness, and wrath, and anger, and clamor, and evil speaking, be put away from you, with all malice: And be ye kind one to another, tenderhearted, forgiving one another, even as God for Christ's sake hath forgiven you* (*Ephesians 4:31, 32*).

The love of God is the key to freedom from anger. Ask God to increase His grace upon you so that you can love your enemies!

HOW TO DEAL WITH ANGER

Read the following scriptural references pertaining to anger:

- Psalm 32:5
- Deuteronomy 32:33
- Nehemiah 9:17
- Psalms 27:9; 30:5; 85:4; 103:8
- Proverbs 15:1
- Isaiah 48:9
- Ecclesiastes 7:9
- Joel 2:13
- Micah 7:18
- Ephesians 4:31
- Colossians 3:8
- James 1:19

Write down what Holy Spirit revealed to you about anger.

_____

_____

_____

_____

_____

_____

_____

_____

List at least two <u>negative</u> emotions that you found in the above scriptures.

_____

_____

_____

_____

_____

_____

_____

List at least two <u>positive</u> emotions that you found in the above scriptures.

_____

_____

_____

_____

_____

_____

_____

What is God's direction to you as it pertains to anger?

_____

_____

_____

_____

_____

_____

_____

_____

What is anger's purpose?

_____

_____

_____

_____

_____

_____

_____

What will anger do if you allow it to remain inside of you?

_____

_____

_____

_____

_____

_____

_____

_____

To begin the deliverance process from anger:

1. <u>Acknowledge your anger.</u> When you face your enemy or that which is a stronghold in your life, it no longer has control over you. Facing it breaks its power over you – ***Praise God!***

2. <u>Accept and Own your Anger.</u> How is anger affecting you?

   Name everyone with whom you are currently angry.

_____

_____

_____

_____

_____

_____

_____

3. <u>Write each Person on your List a Letter.</u> Express what you are feeling at this moment. Explain what they did or said to anger you.

Upon completion of writing letter, you may keep it or destroy it. If at all possible, schedule a meeting or call with those persons and be reconciled.

4. <u>Confess your sin.</u> *I John 1:9* (Amplified) clearly tells us *that if we [freely] admit that we have sinned and confess our sins, He is faithful and just (true to His own nature and promises) and will forgive our sins [dismiss our lawlessness] and [continuously] cleanse us from all unrighteousness [everything not in conformity to His will in purpose, thought and action].* Go on…talk to God about your anger.

5. <u>Trust the Holy Spirit.</u> The Holy Spirit, your Comforter and Guide, our Peace, and Counselor is right there to <u>help</u> you. The Holy Spirit is a Helper. He will give you wisdom, understanding, counsel and might. *Isaiah 40:29* says, *He giveth power to the faint; and to them that have no might He increases strength.*

Remember the Scripture, when we willingly and freely confess our sin, Jesus is faithful to forgive us, release us and remember our sins no more. That means that God will never use our sin against us. *Whom the Son sets free is free indeed (John 8:36).*

6. <u>Consider these questions</u> **to find out if you are angry at God...**

- Do you find yourself asking God "why"?
- Do you pray less than you did in the past?
- Do you attend church less than you did in the past?
- Do you feel a distance or void in your heart when it comes to God?
- Do you read the Bible less than before?

If you answered 'yes' to any one of the preceding questions, you need to acknowledge how you are feeling about God. Examine yourself and ask Him <u>in earnest</u> to speak the truth to you in love about where you are. Remember that He is a merciful God and He loves you more than life. He is lovingly waiting to forgive you, bless you and bring about His plans for your life.

7. <u>Forgive God.</u> There are times when we are angry at God, but wouldn't dare say it. Ask the Holy Spirit to reveal to you if you are holding unforgiveness in your heart toward God or yourself. Ask Him to uncover, reveal, and illuminate anything that is blacked-out, blocked, repressed or suppressed in your subconscious and bring it to your remembrance. If there is anything, go on and

give it to Jesus in prayer. Remember, He is a loving Father who has given you access to Him and one who listens and loves well.

ANGER
PERSONAL REFLECTIONS

NOTES

_____

_____

_____

_____

_____

_____

_____

_____

THOUGHTS / DIRECTION FROM HOLY SPIRIT

_____

_____

_____

_____

_____

_____

_____

_____

PERSONAL ACTION PLAN

_____

_____

_____

_____

_____

_____

_____

_____

Chapter 25

Rejection

"All that the Father giveth me, shall come to me; and him
that cometh to me, I will in no wise reject."
John 6:37 (Webster's Bible Translation)

REJECTION IS A NEGATIVE EMOTION which sets up a mindset that one is incapable of doing or saying anything for fear that others will not accept, affirm or approve of them. Rejection, regardless of the age it begins, is housed in the soul (mind, will, emotions). Most rejection is usually first experienced within the family. This is especially prevalent in the case where there are siblings. Oftentimes one child may feel that the other gets more attention from the parents for a myriad of reasons: intelligence, talents, looks, temperament, sickness, etc.

Please understand that God approves of you and values you...regardless of what others think. Before He formed you in your mother's womb, He had already affirmed, approved and accepted you. (*Jeremiah 1:5*) <u>God placed value and worth on the inside of you!</u> How do I know that? He put Himself (His Holy Spirit) on the inside of you. (*Ephesians 1:13, 14*)

Rejection is a fruit (or symptom) of jealousy, envy or abandonment and it sets up deep inner hurts, resulting in damaged or toxic emotions. In order to get emotionally

healed from rejection, it is critical to go back to the root of the problem and try to pinpoint (as much as possible) when, where and by whom the seed of rejection entered so that the healing process can begin. **Remember…what you do not confront continues to have control and dominion over you.** *Confront and Overcome!*

Here are some of the toxic fruits of rejection. People who feel rejected often display some form of the following behaviors or emotions:

- Aloneness
- Anger
- Anxiety
- Bitterness
- Cares too little or too much about appearance
- Constant worry and doubt of self and others
- Defensive of self and others

- Distant relationship with God
- Envy
- Feelings are easily hurt
- Introverted
- Jealousy
- Lack of trust
- Little or no intrinsic value or self recognition
- Loneliness
- Low self-confidence/worth
- Low self-esteem
- Low self-image
- Needs approval of others
- Perfectionism
- Rebellious behavior
- Shyness
- Withdrawal

REJECTION EXERCISE

1. List the rejection behaviors/emotions that are operating (or have operated) in your life.

2. Take a few seconds to think on each behavior that you have written.

- Can you remember when you first noticed these behaviors operating in your life? Yes No

- Do you know what triggers these emotions or behaviors?   Yes No
- Are there places you don't go or things you don't do because of these negative behaviors or emotions?   Yes No
- Think on each parent and each sibling. Write down their names. Does either of them trigger a negative emotion? (*If yes, write the emotion next to the appropriate name*).

_____

_____

_____

_____

_____

_____

- Think on boyfriends, girlfriends, and ex-husbands/wives. Write down their names. Does either of them trigger a negative emotion? (*If yes, write the emotion next to the appropriate name*)

_____

_____

_____

_____

_____

_____

_____

_____

- Think about a boss (past or present), a friend, a family member, a pastor, a minister, a church member? Does either of them trigger a negative emotion? (*If yes, write their name and the negative emotion next to the appropriate name*)

_____

_____

_____

_____

_____

_____

3. Write down any particular situation, circumstance, or relationship when rejection entered your heart or when you generally felt symptoms of rejection as a child or adult.

_____

_____

_____

_____

_____

_____

_____

_____

4. Compile a list of names by writing the names from numbers 1, 2 and 3. Next to the name, write the form of rejection and the negative emotions or behavior:

<u>Name</u>	<u>Form of Rejection</u>	<u>Negative Emotion</u>
Examples:		
Betty (mom)	**Favored my sister over me**	**Resentment**
John (boss)	**Passed over me for promotion**	**Anger**
XYZ (husband)	**Cheated with another woman**	**Betrayed**

_____

_____

_____

_____

_____

_____

The blood of Jesus has healed (or freed) you from rejection and given you complete acceptance in Him. It is time to ***renounce*** all the negative emotions that you listed. To renounce means to give up claim to, quit, part with, abandon, wash one's hands of, cast aside, put aside, dismiss, reject, and turn from.

5. Write a paragraph (three or more sentences) to each person on the list. Specifically tell them "what" they did or did not do to you and "how you feel." Use words describing your actual feelings.

Example:

Dear Mom,

I am writing to tell you that you hurt me deeply when you sided with my sister over me. You knew she was wrong. I resent you and I resent her. I always felt that you loved her more, now I know for sure. I don't know what to do because I still love you — you are my mother.

I am trying to get some counseling so I will be able to let my resentment, hurt and pain go. It is hard, but I know God does not want me to resent you or disobey you. I hope that we will be able to get past this.

-Betty

Now, write your letters. You may only be able to write one letter at a time. That's okay! Take your time and work at your own pace. When you finish, go to the next page.

Prayer to renounce the negative emotions related to Rejection

Father, I come to You with thanksgiving and praise for Your mercy and grace in my life. I thank You for Your great love towards me. I ask You to forgive me for every sin and the negative emotion of rejection that I allowed to enter into my heart and mind. Forgive me for allowing rejection and its fruit to control, rule and govern my actions and my thoughts. I renounce the spirit of rejection and all of its effects on my life. I replace the negative emotion of rejection with forgiveness, acceptance, love and all the good treasures within me. I receive Your love, acceptance and approval. Heavenly Father, thank You for the plans and purpose You have for my life. I declare that I am fearfully and wonderfully made; I am Your beloved and Your friend; I am deeply loved by You and fully clothed in Your fine, holy garment of righteousness, purchased by the blood of Jesus. I am fully accepted and approved! I am the righteousness of God, in the name of Jesus. **AMEN!**

REJECTION
PERSONAL REFLECTIONS

NOTES

_____

_____

_____

_____

_____

_____

_____

_____

THOUGHTS / DIRECTION FROM HOLY SPIRIT

_____

_____

_____

_____

_____

_____

_____

PERSONAL ACTION PLAN

_____

_____

_____

_____

_____

_____

_____

_____

Chapter 26

Depression

*"To appoint unto them that mourn in Zion, to give unto them beauty for ashes, the oil of joy for mourning, the garment of praise for the spirit of **heaviness**."*

Isaiah 61:3

DEPRESSION IS A PROLONGED FEELING of sadness, discouragement and an inability to "get on top of things." Depression affects one's physical, mental, emotional and spiritual well-being. Depression may be caused by marital problems, loss of a job, major medical conditions, stress, rejection by family, peers and friends, as well as sin, grief and sorrow.

Depression is a complex mental health issue and statistics show that suicide (an effect of depression) is the third leading cause of teenage deaths. More and more elderly people are also experiencing some degree of depression due to reactions to a combination of medicines.

Depression is a biblical word that the Bible describes as *heaviness*. Other biblical descriptions are *blackness* and *darkness*. (See *Jeremiah 8:21, 22* and *Job 3*.)

SOME FACTS ABOUT DEPRESSION:

- Each year about 17 million people in the United States will experience depression.
- Women are at greater risk for depression than men.
- Depression affects every part of the physical body.
- Depression is an illness that affects the body, soul and spirit.
- Depression affects the way you think, feel and act.
- Depression is both psychological and spiritual and may be caused by a chemical imbalance in the brain.

Some symptoms of depression are a *total loss of will, hope, joy, energy and emotional life*. Oftentimes, survivors of depression describe the state of depression as a *black pit* or a *dark hole*. This seemingly indicates a location within them so deep and dark that they are lifeless, hopeless and helpless.

Here are *some* (not all) of the emotions and/or behaviors that lead to depression:

- Anxieties
- Betrayal
- Bitterness
- Death
- Fear
- Grief
- Guilt
- Hatred
- Heaviness
- Loss
- Oppression
- Rejection
- Shame
- Sorrow
- Unmet expectations
- Unresolved conflicts

TYPES OF DEPRESSION

There are several types of depression:

1. <u>Major Depression</u> (also known as clinical depression) – People have some or all of the depression symptoms listed below for at least two weeks, up to several months, or longer:

- Appetite or weight loss, or overeating and weight gain
- Decreased energy and fatigue
- Excessive crying
- Feelings of guilt, worthlessness, helplessness
- Irritability
- Loss of interest in sex
- Loss of interest or pleasure in activities
- Persistent headaches, digestive disorders or chronic pain
- Persistent sadness, anxiety or empty mood
- Sleeping too much or too little
- Thoughts of death or suicide attempts

2. <u>Dysthymia</u> – The same symptoms of major depression are present. However, they are <u>milder</u> but last for at least two years. Major expressive episodes can also be experienced.

3. <u>Manic Depression</u> (also called bipolar disorder) – This type of depression is not as common as other forms of depression. It is characterized by extreme highs and lows, such as euphoria (a feeling of great happiness or well-being; commonly exaggerated and not necessarily well-founded) and great excitement to irritability and rage.

Here are some of the *symptoms of manic depression*:

- Abnormally elevated mood
- Grandiose notions
  Note: *Grandiose* means to have an exaggerated belief in one's importance, sometimes reaching delusional proportions
- Inappropriate social behaviors
- Increased sexual activity
- Risk-taking behaviors
- Severe insomnia

TREATMENT FOR CLINICAL OR MAJOR DEPRESSION

Get professional counseling by a psychologist or psychiatrist. This type of depression will most likely require counseling combined with medication to help relieve physical symptoms.

Depression requires treatment; therefore, if you are experiencing any of the causes of depression or prolonged sadness and discouragement, please get professional counseling to determine the type of treatment needed. Depending on the degree, a pastoral counselor may be a great support in getting to the spiritual root of the problem and facilitating the process of *Inner Healing;* however, you may also require a medical diagnosis and treatment and/or formal counseling.

QUESTIONS ABOUT DEPRESSION (THIS MAY BE ABLE TO HELP YOU DETERMINE IF YOU ARE SUFFERING FROM DEPRESSION)

1. Do you feel as though you are in a *deep dark pit* or a *deep dark hole*?

   Yes   No   Sometimes
   How long have you felt this way?

2. Do you have a total lack of energy?

   Yes   No   Sometimes
   How long have you felt this way?

3. Do you hate to face each day?

   Yes   No   Sometimes
   How long have you felt this way?

4. Do you have difficulty being around people?

   Yes   No   Sometimes
   How long have you felt this way?

5. Do you have difficulty completing daily chores?

   Yes   No   Sometimes
   How long have you felt this way?

6. Do you find yourself sleeping more and more?

   Yes   No   Sometimes
   How long have you felt this way?

7. Do you have moods of extreme highs and extreme lows?

   Yes   No   Sometimes
   How long have you felt this way?

If you answered YES to 2 or more of the questions above, seek professional or pastoral counseling, or a combination of both.

DEPRESSION
PERSONAL REFLECTIONS

NOTES

_____

_____

_____

_____

_____

_____

_____

_____

THOUGHTS / DIRECTION FROM HOLY SPIRIT

_____

_____

_____

_____

_____

_____

_____

_____

PERSONAL ACTION PLAN

_____

_____

_____

_____

_____

_____

_____

_____

Chapter 27

Stress

"Never worry about anything. Instead, in every situation let your petitions be made known to God through prayers and requests, with thanksgiving."

Philippians 4:6

"And the peace of God, which passeth all understanding, shall keep your hearts and minds through Christ Jesus."

Philippians 4:7

STRESS IS THE NON-SPECIFIC RESPONSE of the body to any demand upon it. Stress can be good or bad. It becomes dangerous when it is unduly prolonged, comes too often or concentrates on one organ of the body. Stress is a mental tension or strain, urgency or pressure. Any negative or opposing impact on the mental and physical parts of the body has a negative effect on the spirit, soul, and body of man. Stress not only causes depression, anxiety and panic attacks, but stress is also a *killer* of the soul (mind, will, emotions) if not timely and effectively addressed.

Stress on the body is one of the most destructive forces a person can face and it can lead to depression. Chronic stress affects you physically, mentally, emotionally and spiritually.

STRESS MANIFESTS ITSELF IN THE FOLLOWING WAYS:

- Anxiety
- Discouragement
- Disappointment
- Insomnia
- Impulsive and Compulsive behaviors
- Oppression
- Overeating
- Sleeplessness
- Substance dependence
- Under-eating
- Worry

Here are some *stress reducers*:

- Get a physical exam or talk to your doctor about stress or depression.

- Exercise at least three to four times a week. Walking is a great way to relieve stress while infusing the body with good endorphins (substances produced by the brain that have painkilling and tranquilizing effects on the body).
- Reduce excessive work hours.
- Learn to say *No*.
- Recognize and admit that you are under stress.
- Think positively.
- Take regularly scheduled vacations.
- Practice or participate in your hobbies.
- Schedule some *me* time.
- Laugh, laugh and laugh some more.
- Reduce clutter in the home, especially in the bedroom where you sleep.
- Practice positive meditation.

"Finally, brethren, whatsoever things are true, whatsoever things are honest, whatsoever things are just, whatsoever things are pure, whatsoever things are lovely, whatsoever things are of good report; if there be any virtue, and if there be any praise, think on these things."

Philippians 4:8

MORE *STRESS REDUCERS*:

- Listen to soft music.
- Learn to *let go and let God*.
- Practice relaxing.
- Sing your favorite songs or hymns.
- Pray and release stress to God.

Finally, you should learn your body's stress language. The body sends signals when it is under stress. Listen to your body. It is vitally important that you immediately reduce the stress in your life!

STRESS
PERSONAL REFLECTIONS

NOTES

_____

_____

_____

_____

_____

_____

_____

_____

THOUGHTS / DIRECTION FROM HOLY SPIRIT

_____

_____

_____

_____

_____

_____

_____

PERSONAL ACTION PLAN

_____

_____

_____

_____

_____

_____

_____

_____

Chapter 28

The Key - Forgiveness

*"Your heavenly Father will forgive you if you forgive those
who sin against you."*

Mark 6:14

*"And be ye kind one to another, tenderhearted, forgiving one
another, even as God for Christ's sake hath forgiven you."*

Ephesians 4:32

FORGIVENESS MEANS TO PARDON. GOD has provided
the ultimate pardon for us through the shed Blood
of Jesus Christ, His only-begotten Son. In addition
to God providing the ultimate sacrifice for sin, He also
provided the foundation for absolute "forgiveness" in the
person of Jesus Christ. All of us as people of God find
ourselves eternally indebted to His kindness which leads
to our forgiveness. As believers, we are exhorted to be
kind to <u>believers</u> and <u>unbelievers</u>. We are exhorted to

be kind, tenderhearted and forgiving to one another as God "for Christ's sake hath forgiven you." (Ephesians 4:32). Because we have been so lovingly and graciously forgiven by God, we <u>must</u> lovingly and graciously forgive the believer <u>and</u> the unbeliever.

Forgiveness is a critical key to *Inner Healing* and walking in soul prosperity. Unforgiveness blocks the flow of love and the blessings and promises of God in one's life. It is therefore imperative to quickly forgive those who have offended, abused or caused you great emotional pain. Sometimes it is easier to forgive others than to forgive ourselves. You are God's ***beloved***. You are valuable and worthy to God and others. You must operate and demonstrate your royalty and kingship as a believer. Forgiveness of God, self and others is vital if you want to experience *Inner Healing* and wholeness.

Let's build our faith to forgive by reading and meditating on the following scriptures from the New International Version (NIV) translation of the Bible:

- This, then, is how you should pray: Our Father in heaven, hallowed be your name, your kingdom come, your will be done on earth as it is in heaven. Give us today our daily bread. Forgive us our debts, as we also have forgiven our debtors. And lead us not into temptation, but deliver us from the evil one. For if you forgive men when they sin against you, your heavenly Father will also forgive you. But if you do not forgive men their sins, your Father will not forgive your sins. *Matthew 6:9-15*

- And when you stand praying, if you hold anything against anyone, forgive him, so that your Father in heaven may forgive you your sins. *Mark 11:25*

- Be devoted to one another in brotherly love. Honor one another above yourselves. Live in harmony with one another. Do not be proud, but be willing to associate with people of low position. Do not be conceited. Do not repay anyone evil for evil. Be careful to do what is right in the eyes of everybody. If it is possible, as far as it depends on you, live at peace with everyone. *Romans 12:10, 16-18*

- Give everyone what you owe him: If you owe taxes, pay taxes; if revenue, then revenue; if respect, then respect; if honor, then honor. Let no debt remain outstanding, except the continuing debt to love one another, for he who loves his fellowman has fulfilled the law. *Romans 13:7-8*

- And do not give the devil a foothold. Get rid of all bitterness, rage and anger, brawling and slander, along with every form of malice. Be kind and compassionate to one another, forgiving each other, just as in Christ God forgave you. *Ephesians 4:27, 31, 32*

- Then make my joy complete by being like-minded, having the same love, being one in spirit and purpose. *Philippians 2:2*

- Finally, all of you, live in harmony with one another; be sympathetic, love as brothers, be compassionate and humble. He must turn from evil and do good; he must seek peace and pursue it. For the eyes of the Lord are on the righteous and his ears are attentive to their prayer, but the face of the Lord is against those who do evil. *I Peter 3:8, 11, 12*

PRINCIPLES OF FORGIVENESS

- Forgiveness is a commandment of God.
- Forgiveness is a personal choice.
- Forgiveness is a decision.
- Forgiveness is an act of your free will.
- Forgiveness does not mean ***forgotten***.
- Forgiveness is a positive emotion that is motivated by love.

- Forgiveness is agreeing with the Word of God to live with the consequences of another person's sin.

- The decision to forgive presupposes you may experience some pain of the past.

- You have the power to forgive anyone who hurt, abused or offended you. The God of Love, Jesus our Redeemer and the Sweet Communion of the Holy Spirit are there to enable and empower you to forgive.

PRAYER FOR REPENTANCE AND UNFORGIVENESS

*Father God, I come in the name of
Jesus thanking You for forgiving
me of all my sins. I repent of
unforgiveness and I ask You
to purge and purify my heart. I desire
to have a heart like Yours…
pure, holy, righteous and godly, in Jesus' name.
Create in me a clean heart and
renew a right spirit within me.
I forgive everyone who has hurt,
offended, abused, or abandoned me.
I release them in the name of Jesus.
I ask You to draw them closer to You,
and I thank You for blessing them,
in the name of Jesus. AMEN!*

Forgiveness Exercise

1. **List everyone** you need to forgive (include yourself **and** God if necessary). Go back into your childhood as far as you can remember.

_____

_____

_____

_____

_____

_____

_____

_____

2. **List everyone** who physically, emotionally, sexually, or mentally abused you.

_____

_____

_____

_____

_____

_____

_____

_____

3. Offer your lists (from lists 1 and 2) up to God. Ask God to give you the **grace** (His divine mercy, ability, power, and influence) to forgive and release each person.

"Job's captivity was turned when he prayed for his friends."
Job 42:10

4. Repeat this prayer for <u>each</u> name on your list: God, I forgive (**name the person**) for (**name the offense**). I release (**name the person**) and commend the hurt and (**name the person**) into Your hand. I pray that you will bless (**name the person**) in Jesus' name.

5. **Ask God to forgive you** for holding unforgiveness in your heart against this person (or these people) and to cleanse you with the blood of Jesus.

6. **Thank God for the gift of forgiveness** and the ability to break the power of control the offender/abuser had over you as a result of the offense. Thank God for releasing/delivering you and restoring you back to mental, emotional, and physical health in Jesus' name. Declare that you are **now** free to move into the plans and purposes that God has for your life.

CONGRATULATIONS!

Now walk in the FREEDOM and LIBERTY of the Spirit of God, which He has restored to you this day!

FORGIVENESS
PERSONAL REFLECTIONS

NOTES

_____

_____

_____

_____

_____

_____

_____

_____

THOUGHTS / DIRECTION FROM HOLY SPIRIT

_____

_____

_____

_____

_____

_____

_____

_____

PERSONAL ACTION PLAN

_____

_____

_____

_____

_____

_____

_____

_____

Chapter 29

Accepting Personal Responsibility
in the Healing Process

"If we confess our sins, he is faithful and just to forgive us
our sins, and to cleanse us from all unrighteousness."

I John 1:9

RESPONSIBILITY MEANS THAT ONE IS answerable
and accountable for his choices, decisions and
actions. Responsibility is critical to the healing,
deliverance and restoration process. Personal responsibility
is an individual choice. God has given each of us a free will
to make choices and decisions. We must take ownership
and responsibility for our decisions; regardless of the
circumstances and situations those choices and decisions
create.

ACCEPTING PERSONAL RESPONSIBILITY INCLUDES...

- Acknowledging that you are solely responsible for the choices in your life
- Accepting that you are responsible for what you choose to feel or think
- Accepting that you choose the direction for your life
- Accepting that you cannot blame others for the choices you have made
- Tearing down the mask of defense or rationale for why others are responsible for who you are, what has happened to you, and what you are bound to become
- The rational belief that you are responsible for determining who you are, and how your choices affect your life
- Pointing the finger of responsibility back to yourself and away from others when you are discussing the consequences of your actions
- Realizing that you determine your feelings about any events or actions addressed to you, no matter how negative they seem
- Recognizing that you are your best cheerleader; it is not reasonable or healthy for you to

depend on others to make you feel good about yourself

- Recognizing that as you enter adulthood and maturity, you determine and develop your own self-esteem
- Not feeling sorry for the *bum deal* you have been handed but taking hold of your life and giving it direction and reason
- Letting go of your sense of over responsibility for others
- Protecting and nurturing your health and emotional well-being
- Taking preventive health-oriented steps of structuring your life with time management, stress management, confronting fears and burnout prevention
- Taking an honest inventory of your strengths, abilities, talents, virtues, and positive points
- Developing positive, self-affirming, self-talk scripts to enhance your personal development and growth
- Letting go of blame and anger toward those in your past who did the best they could, given the limitations of their knowledge, background, and awareness

When you have not accepted personal responsibility, you run the risk of becoming...

- Overly dependent on others for recognition, approval, affirmation and acceptance
- Chronically hostile, angry, or depressed over how unfairly you have been or are being treated
- Fearful about ever taking a risk or making a decision
- Overwhelmed by disabling fears
- Unsuccessful at the enterprises you take on in life
- Unsuccessful in personal relationships
- Emotionally or physically unhealthy
- Addicted to unhealthy substances, such as the abuse of alcohol, drugs, food, or unhealthy behavior such as excessive gambling, shopping, sex, smoking, work, etc.
- Overly responsible and guilt-ridden in your need to rescue and enable others
- Unable to develop trust or to feel secure with others
- Resistant to vulnerability

WHAT PEOPLE BELIEVE WHEN THEY DON'T TAKE PERSONAL RESPONSIBILITY...

- It's not my fault I am the way I am
- I never asked to be born
- Now that you have me, what are you going to do with me?
- I want you to fix me
- Life is unfair! There is no sense in trying to take control of my life.
- Why go on? I see no use in it.
- You can't help me, nobody can help me. I'm useless and a failure.
- God has asked too much of me this time. There is no way I'll ever be able to handle this.
- When do the troubles and problems cease? I'm tired of all this.
- Stop the world; I want to get off.
- Life is so depressing. If only I had better luck and had been born to a healthier family, or attended a better school, or gotten a better job, etc.
- How can you say I am responsible for what happens to me in the future? There is fate, luck, politics, greed, envy, wicked and jealous people, and other negative influences that

have a greater bearing on my future than I have.

- How can I ever be happy, seeing how bad my life has been?
- My parents made me what I am today!
- The problems in my family have influenced who I am and what I will be; there is nothing I can do to change that.
- Racism, bigotry, prejudice, sexism, ageism and closed mindedness all stand in the way of my becoming what I really want to be.
- No matter how hard I work, I will never get ahead.
- You have to accept the luck of the draw.
- I am who I am; there is no changing me.
- No one is going to call me crazy, depressed, or troubled and then try to change me.

BEHAVIOR TRAITS THAT ENABLE YOU TO ACCEPT PERSONAL RESPONSIBILITY...

- Seek out and accept help for yourself.
- Be open to new ideas or concepts about life and the human condition.
- Refute irrational beliefs and overcome fears.
- Positively affirm yourself.
- Recognize that you are the sole determinant of the choices you make.

- Recognize that you choose your responses to the people, actions and events in your life.
- Let go of anger, fear, blame, mistrust and insecurity.
- Take risks and become vulnerable to change and growth in your life.
- Take off the masks of behavior characteristics behind which you hide low self-esteem.
- Re-organize your priorities and goals.
- Realize that you are in charge of the direction your life takes.

STEPS NECESSARY TO ACCEPT PERSONAL RESPONSIBILITY...

Step 1: Answer the following questions to determine if you are having problems accepting personal responsibility:

- How frequently do you claim that others have determined what you are today?
- How easy is it to accept that you are responsible for your choices in life?
- How easy it is to believe that you determine the direction your life takes?
- How easy is it to blame others for where you are today?
- What masks do you hide behind to avoid accepting personal responsibility?

- How rational are you in dealing with the part you played in being who you are today?
- How easy is it to accept blame or admit mistakes?
- How easy is it to accept that you determine your feelings when negative events occur?
- How easy is it to solely depend on you for acceptance, affirmation and approval?
- How willing are you to be the sole determinant of the health of your self-esteem?
- How frequently do you feel sorry for yourself?
- How willingly do you take preventive steps to ensure your physical and emotional health?
- How successfully have you practiced self-affirmation in your life?

Step 2: Use the following scale of 1 to 5 to assess your level of personal responsibility in the following areas of your life...

1 = always irresponsible

2 = usually irresponsible

3 = irresponsibility balanced out with responsibility (neutral)

4 = usually responsible

5 = always responsible

Taking the preventive and maintenance measures to ensure physical health

Taking the preventive and maintenance measures to ensure emotional health

Controlling weight and over-eating

Stopping smoking, excessive drinking and drug abuse

Controlling excessive gambling, shopping and sexual behavior

Controlling workaholism

Taking the preventative and maintenance measures to ensure healthy relationships

Taking the necessary steps to overcome current problems and troubles

Taking the necessary steps to protect yourself from being victimized by your rescuing and enabling of others

Managing your time, managing the stress in your life, overcoming your fears, and preventing burnout in your life

A rating of 3 or less in any of the areas indicates a need to accept personal responsibility.

Step 3: Identify your beliefs that prevent acceptance of responsibility for yourself. Develop new, rational, replacement beliefs to help you accept responsibility for yourself.

Step 4: You are now ready to develop a plan of action. For each area of your life, identify what you will do to accept personal responsibility. Be sure to date and sign your plan.

Step 5: If you still have trouble accepting personal responsibility, seek additional help such as finding a mentor or someone you trust to hold you accountable.

ACCEPTING RESPONSIBILITY IN THE HEALING PROCESS
PERSONAL REFLECTIONS

NOTES

A rating of 3 or less in any of the areas indicates a need to accept personal responsibility.

_____

_____

_____

_____

_____

_____

_____

THOUGHTS / DIRECTION FROM HOLY SPIRIT

_____

_____

_____

_____

_____

_____

_____

PERSONAL ACTION PLAN

_____

_____

_____

_____

_____

_____

_____

_____

Chapter 30

Who We Are In Christ

"Therefore if any man be in Christ, he is a new creature: old things are passed away; behold, all things are become new."

II Corinthians 5:17

THE WORD OF GOD HAS MUCH to say about who we are in Christ. Use the following scriptures to meditate on all the benefits that belong to those who are born again in Christ Jesus. The knowledge and confidence of your ability and power in Him is key to walking in *Inner Healing* and wholeness.

Who I Am...

One who walks in dominion and authority

How do I Know...

And God blessed them, and God said unto them, be fruitful, and multiply, and replenish the earth, and subdue it: and have dominion over the fish of the sea, and over the fowl of the air, and over every living thing that moveth upon the earth.

(*Genesis 1:28*)

The head and not the tail; above ONLY and NEVER beneath

And the LORD shall make thee the head, and not the tail; and thou shalt be above only, and thou shalt not be beneath; if that thou hearken unto the commandments of the LORD thy God, which I command thee this day, to observe and to do them.

(*Deuteronomy 28:13*)

The Apple of His eye	He found him in a desert land, and in the waste howling wilderness; he led him about, he instructed him, he kept him as the apple of his eye.
	(Deuteronomy 32:10)
Blessed – sacred, holy, favored, and fortunate	Blessed are they which are persecuted for righteousness' sake: for theirs is the kingdom of heaven. Blessed are ye, when men shall revile you, and persecute you, and shall say all manner of evil against you falsely, for my sake. Rejoice, and be exceeding glad: for great is your reward in heaven: for so persecuted they the prophets which were before you. *(Matthew 5:10-12)*

Loved	For God so loved the world, that he gave his only begotten Son, that whosoever believeth in him should not perish, but have everlasting life. (*John 3:16*)
Friend – an associate whom one likes	Henceforth I call you not servants; for the servant knoweth not what his lord doeth: but I have called you friends; for all things that I have heard of my Father I have made known unto you. (*John 15:15*)

One who walks in ability, efficiency, and might	But ye shall receive power, after that the Holy Ghost is come upon you: and ye shall be witnesses unto me both in Jerusalem, and in all Judaea, and in Samaria, and unto the uttermost part of the earth. (*Acts 1:8*)
Overcomer	Nay, in all these things we are more than conquerors through him that loved us. (*Romans 8:37*)
A new creation in Christ and a minister of reconciliation	Therefore if any man be in Christ, he is a new creature: old things are passed away; behold all things are become new. And all things are of God, who hath reconciled us to himself by Jesus Christ, and hath given to us the ministry of reconciliation. (*II Corinthians 5:17,18*)

An Ambassador for Christ	Now then we are ambassadors for Christ, as though God did beseech you by us: we pray you in Christ's stead, be ye reconciled to God. (*II Corinthians 5:20*)
A Saint	Paul, an apostle of Jesus Christ by the will of God, to the saints which are at Ephesus, and to the faithful in Christ Jesus. (*Ephesians 1:1*)
His workmanship	For we are his workmanship, created in Christ Jesus unto good works, which God hath before ordained that we should walk in them. (*Ephesians 2:10*)

A fellow citizen in the Kingdom	Now therefore ye are no more strangers and foreigners, but fellow citizens with the saints, and of the household of God.
	(*Ephesians 2:19*)
Redeemed	In whom we have redemption through his blood, even the forgiveness of sins.
	(*Colossians 1:14*)
Complete in Christ	And ye are complete in him, which is the head of all principality and power:.
	(*Colossians 2:10*)

A Chosen Generation and Royal Priesthood	But ye are a chosen generation, a royal priesthood, an holy nation, a peculiar people; that ye should shew forth the praises of him who hath called you out of darkness into his marvelous light.
	(*I Peter 2:9*)
Beloved – deeply and completely loved	Beloved, I wish above all things that thou mayest prosper and be in health, even as thy soul prospereth.
	(*3 John 2*)

CONFESSIONS
I am Deeply Loved...

ACCEPTED
I am totally Acceptable and Accepted...

And although you were formerly alienated and hostile in mind, engaged in evil deeds, yet He has now reconciled you in His fleshly body through death, in order to present you before Him holy and blameless and beyond reproach.

(Colossians 1:21-22)

BELOVED

I am not Condemned

There is therefore now no condemnation to them which are in Christ Jesus, who walk not after the flesh, but after the spirit.

(Romans 8:1)

Now that you have the knowledge of who you are in Christ, you can continue to build your faith by speaking (or confessing) what God has said about *you* in His Word! You are what you say. The Word of God declares that there is power and death in the tongue. We can **speak** life or death. Choose life!

More Scripture References for Who You are In Christ

I AM In Christ

I am: God's child for I am born again of the incorruptible seed of the Word of God. *1 Peter 1:23*

I am: Forgiven of all my sins and washed in the Blood. *Ephesians 1:7, Hebrews 9:14; Colossians 1:14, 1 John 1:9*

I am: A new creature in Christ. *2 Corinthians 5:17*

I am: The temple of the Holy Spirit. *1 Corinthians 6:19*

I am: Delivered from the power of darkness and translated in God's kingdom. *Colossians 1:13*

I am: Redeemed from the curse of the law of sin and death. *1 Peter 1:18-19, Galatians 3:13*

I am: Blessed. *Deuteronomy 28:2-12, Galatians 3:9*

I am: A Saint. *Romans 1:7, I Corinthians 1:3, Philippians 1:1*

I am: The head and not the tail, above and not beneath. *Deuteronomy 28:13*

I am: Holy and without blame before Him in Love. *1 Peter 1:16, Ephesians 1:4*

I am: The Elect of God. *Colossians 3-12, Romans 8:33*

I am: Established to the end. *Romans 1:11*

I am: Made near to My Heavenly Father by the Blood of Christ. *Ephesians 2:13*

I am: Set FREE. *John 8:31-33*

I am: Strong in the Lord. *Ephesians 6:10*

I am: Dead to sin. *Romans 6:1, 11 and 1 Peter 2:24*

I am: More than a conqueror. *Romans 8:37*

I am: Joint heir with Christ. *Romans 8:13*

I am: Sealed with the Holy Spirit of promise. *Ephesians 1:13*

I am: In Christ by His doing. *1 Corinthians 1:30*

I am: Accepted in the Beloved. *Ephesians 1:6*

I am: Complete in Him. *Colossians 2:10*

I am: Crucified with Christ. *Galatians 2:20*

I am: Alive with Christ. *Galatians 2:20*

I am: Free from condemnation. *John 5:24*

I am: Reconciled to God. *2 Corinthians 5:18*

I am: Qualified to share in His inheritance. *Colossians 1:12*

I am: Firmly rooted, built up, established in my faith and overflowing with thanksgiving. *Colossians 2:7*

I am: Born of God and the evil one cannot touch me. *1 John 5:18*

I am: His faithful follower. *Revelation 17:14, Ephesians 5:1*

I am: A fellow citizens with the saints of the household of God. *Ephesians 2:19*

I am: Built upon the foundation of the apostles and prophets, Jesus Christ Himself being the chief corner stone. *Ephesians 2:20*

I am: Overtaken with blessings. *Deuteronomy 28:3, Ephesians 1: 3*

I am: His disciple because I have love for others. *John 13:34-35*

I am: The light of the world. *Matthew 5:14*

I am: The salt of the earth. *Matthew 5:13*

I am: The righteousness of God. *2 Corinthians 5:21, 1 Peter 2:24*

I am: A partaker of His Divine Nature. *2 Peter 1:4*

I am: Called of God *2 Timothy 1:9*

I am: An ambassador for Christ. *2 Corthinians 5:20*

I am: God's workmanship created in Christ Jesus for good works. *Ephesians 2:10*

I am: The apple of my Father's eye. *Deuteronomy 32:10*

I am: Healed by the stripes of Jesus. *1 Peter 2:25, Isaiah 53:6*

I am: Being changed into His image. *2 Corinthians 3:18, Philippians 1:6*

I am: A child of God. *John 1:12, Romans 8:16*

I am: Christ friends. *John 15:15*

I am: Chosen and appointed by God to bear His fruit. *John 15:16*

I am: Enslaved to God. *Romans 6:22*

I am: A son/daughter of God. *Romans 8:14-15, Galatians 3:26 and 4:6*

I am: A temple of God. His Spirit dwells in me. *1 Corinthians 3:16, 6:19*

I am: Joined to the Lord and I am one with him. *1 Corinthians 6:17*

I am: A member of Christ's Body. *1 Corinthians 12:27, Ephesians 5:30*

I am: Reconciled to God and I am a minister of reconciliations. *2 Corinthians 5:18-19*

I am: One in Christ. *Galatians 3:26, 28*

I am: An heir of God since I am son/daughter of God. *Galatians 4:6-7*

I am: Righteous and holy. *Ephesians 4:24*

I am: A citizen of Heaven and seated in Heaven right now. *Philippians 3:20, Ephesians 2:6*

I am: An expression of the Life of Christ because He is my life. *Colossians 3:4*

I am: Chosen and dearly loved Christ. *Ephesians 1:4*

I am: A son/daughter of light and not of darkness. *1 Thessalonians 5:5*

I am: A Holy brother/sister, partaker of a Heavenly Calling. *Hebrews 3:1*

I am: One of God's living stones and I am being brought up as a spiritual house. *1 Peter 2:5*

I am: A Chosen Race, a Royal Priesthood, a Holy Nation, A people for God's own possession to proclaim the excellence of Him. *1 Peter 2:9-10*

I am: The enemy of the Devil. *1 Peter 5-8*

I am: Now a child of God, I will resemble Christ when He returns. *1 John 3:1-2*

I am: Not the great I AM but by the grace of God I am what I am. *1 Corinthians 15:10*

I am: Justified, completely forgiven and made righteous. *Romans 5:1*

I am: Dead with Christ and dead to the power of sin's rule over my life. *Romans 5:1-6*

I am: Dead, I no longer live for myself but for God. *2 Corinthians 5:14-15*

I am: Bought with a price, I am not my own, I belong to God. *1 Corinthians 6:19-20*

I am: Established, anointed and sealed by God in Christ. *2 Corinthians 1:21*

I am: Given the Holy Spirit as a pledge, a guarantee of my inheritance. *Ephesians 1:13-14*

I am: Crucified with Christ and it is no longer I who live, but Christ. *Galatians 2:20*

I am: Chosen in Christ before the foundation of the world. *Ephesians 1:4*

I am: Predestined (determined by God) to be a son/daughter. *Ephesians 1:5*

I am: Sanctified and I am one with the Sanctifier, Christ, He is not ashamed to call me brother/sister. *Hebrew 2:11*

I have: Received the Spirit of God into my life that I might know the things given to me by God. *1 Corinthians 2:12*

I have: Been redeemed, forgiven and I am a recipient of His lavish grace. *Ephesians 1:7*

I have: Been raised up and seated with Christ in the Heavenlies. *Ephesians 2:6*

I have: Christ Himself in me. *Colossians 1:27*

I have: Been firmly rooted in Christ and I am now built up in Him. *Colossians 2:7*

I have: Been buried, raised and made alive with Christ. *Colossians 2:12-13*

I have: Been raised up with Christ, my life is now hidden with Christ in God. For Christ is now my life. *Colossians 3:1-4*

I have: Been given a spirit of power, love and self discipline. *2 Timothy 1:7*

I have: Been saved and called (set apart) according to God's doing. *2 Timothy 1:9*

I have: A right to come boldly before the throne to find mercy and grace in time of need. *Hebrews 4:16*

I have: Been given exceedingly great and precious promises by God which I am a partaker of His Divine Nature. *2 Peter 1:4*

I have: The mind of Christ. *Philippians 2:5, 1 Corinthians 2:16*

I have: Obtained an inheritance. *Ephesians 1:11*

I have: Overcome the world. *1 John 5:4*

I can: Do all things in Christ. *Philippians 4:13*

I shall: Overcome because greater is He who is me then he that is in the world. *1 John 4:4*

WHO WE ARE IN CHRIST
PERSONAL REFLECTIONS

NOTES

_____

_____

_____

_____

_____

_____

_____

THOUGHTS / DIRECTION FROM HOLY SPIRIT

_____

_____

_____

_____

_____

_____

_____

PERSONAL ACTION PLAN

_____

_____

_____

_____

_____

_____

_____

_____

End notes

CHAPTER 1

3 John 2
3 John 2
Philippians 2:12
Ephesians 4:12-14
John 10:7;
John 14:6
Hebrews 4:16
Exodus 25-27
James 1:22-25
Ephesians 5:26
Joshua 1:8
I Cor. 13
Isaiah 6:5:
Philippians 2:12

Mark 15:37,38

Colossians 3:3

Proverbs 23:7

Romans 7:25

CHAPTER 2

3 John 2

Philippians 2:5

Philippians 2:8

Ephesians 4:11-20

I John 2:15, 16

Eph. 4:22

Eph. 4:24

I John 2:15

Rom 8:15, 23

Eph 1:5

II Cor 5:17

Heb 8:18; 10:16

Col 2:11

John 3:3

Eph 4:22-24

3 John 2

Romans 7:18

Romans 8:5-8

Rom 8:13

Romans 12:1

Colossians 3:10

Isaiah 14:12-14

Galatians 5:22-23

Romans 12:1-1

Philippians 4:8

Romans 12:2

Philippians 4-8

CHAPTER 3

II Samuel 3:19

Job 3:20

Job 3:21

Genesis 37

Genesis 4:3-8

Ephesians 4:31

Hebrews 12:15

Genesis 4 and Genesis 27

Proverbs 15:13

Matthews 6

Romans 8:1

CHAPTER 4

Genesis 2:18

Genesis 1:27

Genesis 1:28

Galatians 5:19-21

Hebrews 4:16

Chapter 5

The Bait of Satan by John Bevere, published 9/1/03

Luke 17:1

Matthew 22:37-39

I John 5:3

John 13:34

Galatians 5:16-17

Galatians 5:22-23

Proverbs 4:23

James 1:19; 3:5-6

Proverbs 15:1

II Corinthians 10:3-5

Ephesians 4:13

Chapter 6

Work cited:

www.pcar.org/about_sa/stats.html (1 and 4 raped)

www.ojp.usdoj.gov/ovc/.../infoes/.../sexualassaultvictimization.txt (forceable rape)

II Samuel 13

Psalm 139:4

Chapter 7

Proverbs 13:12

Psalm 147:3

Isaiah 53:5

II Timothy 1:7

II Corinthians 5:17

II Samuel 13: 22-23; 28

Romans 12:18

Ephesians 4:26

Ephesians 4:31-32

Pg. 98 (list of scriptures need to list)

I John 1:9

Isaiah 40:29

John 8:36

Jeremiah 1:5

Ephesians 1:13-14

Pg. 111 (cite pharmaceutical television ad "where depression hurts)

Jeremiah 8:21-22

Job 3

Isaiah 61:3

Philippians 4:8

CHAPTER 9

Galatians 5:6

Hebrews 11:6

I Corinthians 13:4-8; 13

John 14:15

I John 5:3

Galatians 5:14

John 15:11

I Corinthians 13

John 15:12-13, 17

Chapter 10

Ephesians 4:32

Matthew 6:19-15 (NIV) transalation bible

Mark 11:25

Romans 12:10, 16-18

Romans 13: 7-8

Ephesians 4:27, 31-32

Philippians 2:2

I Peters 3:8, 11-12

Job 42:10

Chapter 11

Genesis 1:28

Deut 28:13

Deut 32:10

John 3:16

John 15:15

Acts 1:8

Romans 8:37

II Cor. 5:17-18

II Cor 5:20

Ephesians 1:1

Ephesians 2:10

Ephesians 2:19

Col 1:14

Col 2:10

I Peter 2:9

3 John 2

I John 4:9-11

Colossians 1:21-22

Romans 8:1

Chapter 12

Hebrews 4:12

John 14:14

Psalm 66:18

Mark 11:25

Matthew 6:14-15

Romans 10:13

Hebrews 13:21

Isaiah 54:17

Hebrews 4:12 (amplified bible)

Mathew 16:19 (amplified bible)

Mark 11:23-24

Page 156 (list all the scriptures)

Chapter 13

Acts 27:23)

Exodus 12:13)

(Romans 4:3)

Hebrews 11:1)

(Isaiah 58:6

(Acts 1:8)

I Corinthians 13

(John 14:13,14)

(1 Samuel 15:22)

Psalm 100

Matthew 6:5-15

(Mark 11:23)

(Mark 11:14

(Hebrews 4:12)

(Isaiah 55:11)

(Isaiah 11:2)

(James 3:17)

CHAPTER 14

Ephesians 6:10-18 (Amplified):

Hebrew 4:16

Habakkuk 2:2,3

Proverbs 29:18

Pg. 174 I Timothy 4:12; Hebrews 9:14; Romans 2: 14, 15)

Roget's Desk Thesaurus; Gramercy p.349

"*I Am In Christ*," pp. 175-180, <u>Prayers</u>, 10th Edition, Christian Word Ministries, 428 Sutherland Drive, Lexington, Ky 40503, Edition 10.

Work Cited

Robert Todd Carroll, *The Skeptic's Dictionary* (John Wiley & Sons, 2003)

Stephen D. Renn, *Expository Dictionary of Bible Words* (Hendrickson Publishers, 2005)

Roget, *Roget's Desk Thesaurus* (Gramercy Books, Random House, Inc, New York, 1995)

James Strong, *The Strong's Concise Concordance of the Bible* (Thomas Nelson Publishers, Nashville, TN, 1985)

Frank Charles Thompson, *The Thompson Comprehensive Bible Helps, King James Version* (The B.B. Kirkbride Bible Company, Inc, Indianapolis, IN, 1982)

Frank Charles Thompson, *Thompson Chain Reference Study Bible, New International Version, Second Improved Edition*

(The B.B. Kirkbride Bible Company, Inc, Indianapolis, IN, 1990)

Tyndale, *The Life Recovery Bible* (Tyndale House Publishers, Inc, Wheaton, IL, 1998)

Merrill F. Unger, *Unger's Bible Dictionary, 3rd Edition* (Moody Press, Chicago, IL, 1985)

Webster, *Webster's New World Dictionary of the American Language, 2nd College Edition* (Simon and Schuster, 1986)

Wikipedia Foundation, Inc. http:/en.wikipedia.org/wiki

Ronald F. Youngblood, *Nelson's Quick Reference Bible Concordance* (Thomas Nelson Publishers, Nashville, TN, 1993)

Finkelhor and Browne, 1986. http://www.google.com

"Accepting Personal Responsibility", by James J. Messina, PhD. http://www.livestrong.com/article/14698-accepting-personal-responsibility/

John and Paula Sanford, *Healing the Wounded Spirit* (Bridge Publishing, Inc, 1985)

John Bevere, The Bait of Satan-Living Free From the Deadly Trap of Offense (Charisma House, Revised Edition, 2004) USA

The Christian Counseling Handbook, The Topical Handbook used by prayer Counselors, The Christian Broadcasting Network, Virginia Beach, Virgin (Tyndale House Publishers, Inc., Wheaton, Illinois, 1987) US

www.pcar.org/about_sa/stats.html (1 and 4 raped)

www.ojp.usdoj.gov/ovc/.../infoes/.../
sexualassaultvictimization.txt (forceable rape)